THE WOMEN *of* MOLISE

An Italian Village, 1950

THE WOMEN *of* MOLISE

An Italian Village, 1950

words and pictures by

Frank Monaco

FOUR SEASONS
PUBLISHING

Published in England by

FOUR SEASONS
PUBLISHING

16 ORCHARD RISE, KINGSTON UPON THAMES, SURREY, KT2 7EY

Designed in association with

THE BRIDGEWATER BOOK COMPANY

Photographs printed by Albert Boulton

Printed in Singapore

Text and Photographs © 2000 Frank Monaco

ISBN 1 85645 145 3

also by Frank Monaco

They Dwell in Monasteries

For Lavinia, my wife

and

Frank & Elizabeth Selby, founders of Rex Features

INTRODUCTION

This introduction has been adapted from an article written in 1959 by the late Norman Hall, former picture editor of The Times *newspaper, London. At that time he was editor of* Photography *magazine. Seeing the photographs Monaco had taken of the village, he was very keen to publish a selection of them. He wrote the accompanying article. Monaco and Hall were to become lifelong friends.*

★ ★ ★

IN THE WHOLE of Italy there is no province quite like the Molise. It is a wild region, mountainous and largely untamed, an area where the climate is harsh and living is hard. It has always seemed to be detached from the outside world, undeveloped and, in parts, unknown.

Back in the days when Naples was a rich and powerful kingdom it was a declared policy to leave the Molise region, backing on its borders, alone in its primitive state. It was forbidding and untraversable, a natural barrier against invaders. Before then, and since, such a policy has been well suited to the adjoining states and this has helped to generate a feeling of isolation which is both spiritual and physical.

For centuries there were no roads, and even today communications with the world outside seem strangely incomplete. Time brought few changes, and new thoughts and cultures were slow to penetrate. Old customs remained and pagan superstitions lingered on as integral parts of the hard and frugal lives of the inhabitants.

Life has always been like that. This is a hungry country and backward. From Molise there is a steady flow of emigrants to the new worlds of America, Canada and Australia. The men go first, the breadwinners, and they sell their strength wherever and however it is required. Sometimes it will take years before they have saved enough to pay the fares for their womenfolk. The women wait behind, and work, and pray. In the villages there are mothers without sons, sisters without brothers and wives without husbands. The men who remain are either old and spent or mere striplings.

When Frank Monaco was a little boy in New York, his mother told him stories of Cantalupo, the village in the Molise from which she had emigrated as a young woman. He listened, and asked for more with a curiosity that was insatiable. For his mother this was an ease from the longing for old friends and lost surroundings. Monaco knew about almost everyone in the village before he was nine. As soon as he could write, his mother made him address her letters for her and he began to feel he had some physical contact with this strange and wonderful country far away. As he grew older he came to feel his mother's longing to return.

The Second World War brought him to Europe and sent him home again with a right hand that had been badly mauled. After four years he left a career in advertising for a chance to study art and went to Rome under the G.I. Bill for Veterans. Almost immediately he went to

Cantalupo, where there are sixteen Monacos buried in the local churchyard. He was welcomed, not as a visitor but as a returning son.

This was in 1950 and from then on he spent more time in the village than in Rome. He felt completely at peace there and everything was exactly as he had imagined it would be.

On the advice of Afro, one of the leading painters in Italy, Frank Monaco became a photographer. It started with pictures which he took in Cantalupo to send back to his mother. Then others made demands for pictures to be sent to sweethearts, husbands and sons. There was not a family in the village who did not have at least one of its male members abroad. With Monaco they were not self-conscious. They accepted him and trusted him as one of themselves. He photographed the village at work in the fields, at peace in their homes and at prayer in the old stone church. He photographed weddings and christenings and death. In Cantalupo they have their own special feast in August and each year at this time he found his way back there to record the happenings.

These are the photographs in this book. The pictures are simple and intimate glimpses which add up to a record of Monaco's childhood dreams. For his mother, they were more than memories and they encouraged her to make a trip back to Cantalupo to see her birthplace and the friends of her childhood.

ON MY FIRST JOURNEY to Cantalupo, I had a front seat on the early morning bus, and as we moved out of Rome, through a gateway of its ancient wall, I glanced across the aisle at a Carabiniere – carbine slung over his shoulder – sitting behind the driver.

There was hardly any traffic back in 1950 and before long we were on the Via Casilina. The Via Casilina, connecting Rome and Naples by way of Cassino, and used by the Roman legions 2500 years ago, was known as 'Highway 6' to the Allied armies in their advance to Rome during the Second World War.

At the outskirts of Rome, the Carabiniere stood his carbine between his knees and lit a cigarette. As we went along, escorted by roadside slabs that marked the kilometers from Rome, I recalled the story of my grandfather who had served as a Carabiniere in Italy's national police force.

After completing his service, he and grandmother emigrated to America before the turn of the century. However, not long after their arrival, life in the New World came to an end when an accident on a hunting trip left grandfather with a permanently disabled shoulder. No longer able to support his wife and new-born baby, he wrote a letter to the King of Italy and, addressing him as General of Carabinieri, asked for assistance to bring his family back to Cantalupo.

As in a story beginning with 'Once upon a time', a letter arrived from the King expressing sympathy and enclosing funds for the return passage. Back in Cantalupo, good fortune was in store for them; they became the owners of a tavern and raised a family that numbered seven daughters and a son.

Moving through the broad Liri valley, I saw the white ruins of the bombed Benedictine abbey on Monte Cassino that was being rebuilt stone by stone to its original design. Since it was founded in 529, the abbey has suffered destruction by Lombards, Saracens, earthquake and, for the fourth time, during the battles of Cassino.

Below the abbey, a new town was rising from its ruins, although the leftovers of war were everywhere. There were posters on walls with illustrations of shells, grenades and mines: *Non Si Tocca!* (Don't Touch!), the posters warned. I looked into a scrap-metal yard next to the bus station, with its heaps of shrapnel-torn helmets, bits of machine guns, shell casings and tank treads. More than 50,000 Allied and enemy soldiers lost their lives in the four battles of Cassino. And for years the bones of men were unearthed as the farmers ploughed the fields within sight of the British, Polish, French, German and Italian war cemeteries.

Fewer passengers boarded the bus after the refreshment stop, and when the Carabiniere took his place behind the driver we were on our way. A few kilometers outside of Cassino, we left the Via Casilina where it turned for Naples and took a provincial road, narrow and unpaved, that began a zig-zag ascent towards the top of a high ridge.

The climb, in straining low gear and with warning blasts of the klaxon, was slow and dusty as the driver worked hard, taking the turns up the barren slope where not a man nor animal was to be seen. Not far from the crest and by an outcrop of rock, I saw a

marble grave marker adorned with a wreath. The Carabiniere touched the peak of his cap, others made the sign of the Cross. It was there that a traveller was stopped by bandits, robbed and murdered. That was why the armed Carabiniere rode the bus in those days.

On the crest of the ridge a huge wooden cross, silhouetted against the sky, greeted us before we began our descent with an horizon-wide view of mountains, valleys and hill-top villages. We had arrived in the Abruzzi-Molise region, one of the largest and poorest in the country: 6380 square miles with a population of 1,480,000.

Soon, we were in an area with fewer towns and villages. Distances between stops became longer but the roadside slabs continued to measure the kilometers to Rome.

It was when we arrived in the large town of Isernia that I knew Cantalupo was not far away. Isernia, after the surrender of Italy in the war, was bombed by Allied planes. There was not a single military reason for the air bombardment and more than 3000 inhabitants were killed. They said that it was a military error. Forty-two years later, the people of Isernia erected a monument in memory of those killed because of that tragic mistake.

The roadside slab outside Isernia was marked 'Cantalupo, 18 kilometers'. With each turn in the winding road, the countryside appeared to become gentler and lovelier. We passed kerchiefed women working in the fields, many wearing pleated skirts and laced-up sandals with white cotton wrappings to protect their legs in the stubble. The klaxon heralded our approach, telling the farmer to look up and the shepherd to swing his staff at his nervous animals. Finally, the road rose and fell between tall poplars before it levelled off, and with three blasts of the klaxon we came to a stop. I got off the bus with my bag and painting kit. The journey was over.

★ ★ ★

FOR THE FIRST FEW DAYS after my arrival, the childhood remembrances of my mother's longing for her village and youthful past allowed her to appear in all my observations.

What would the American nephew like for his very first breakfast?

He asked for that which his mother had given to him as a child – as rustic as any *colazione* to be had in an Abruzzi kitchen – the yolk of an egg in a glass of wine and a slice of prong-toasted bread. There was a delightful response... Grandfather used to have the very same

colazione; had it been winter, the egg would have been whisked into a bowl of coffee. The American nephew knew that, the whisked egg had been given to him too.

Watching the children as they took the village road up to the old school house, I found myself searching among them for a resemblance of my mother. Again, one afternoon, I went to *la fontana*. The fountain stood in a shallow basin of granite next to the ruins of an old mill. Unobserved, I watched a little girl – ah! the resemblance was there – curl and loop her kerchief, place it on her head and, with a quick movement, lift the jug to rest on her head, and walk gracefully away.

So it was, all that I saw and heard yielded to my mother's presence, until one day, while on a walk in the countryside, I encountered a young girl with a goat and sheep in the stubbled field. I greeted her but my greeting was ignored as her eyes followed me with an unblinking expression. It was then, in the non-response of that encounter – when eagerly looking for the resemblance – that my childhood impressions were put aside for the awareness of the moment.

* * *

CANTALUPO: ELEVATION 468 METERS, population 1900. According to ancient documents, its name comes from the Greek expression Kata lycon – in the locality of the wolf. In the mayor's office, the coat of arms in blue, green and gold shows a wolf in nonchalant passage before a background of mountains. In Italian, Cantalupo means singing wolf.

From the bus stop the village was uphill, an easy kilometer away on a dirt road that acquired tarmac and respectability as it became the main street and entered the piazza. As in all villages, the piazza was the heart of Cantalupo. Quadrangular in shape, modest in size and paved with cobblestones, there you found the priest in his church, the doctor at his pharmacy and the lawyer in his study.

Don Giuseppe di Gregorio – Don Peppino – is the priest, has been all these years. It was after I turned to photography, gave my paintbrushes and tubes of paint to an itinerant painter working on a fresco in the church, that he and I began to get to know each other. A new fresco, to be completed before the *festa*, had been commissioned. 'Take photographs of the fresco and the *festa*', said Don Peppino, pouring

a glass of wine and tossing a pack of American cigarettes on the table. 'I'll have postcards made of the photographs and send them to the Cantalupese in America, Canada, Australia, everywhere. They will send dollars to pay for the fresco, eh! Give me beautiful pictures', he added, 'and I'll pray to St Catherine to help you in your new art!' Don Peppino did not mince words.

I remember a winter Sunday in church when national elections were taking place. Stalin, alive then, was known as *il Baffone* ('the big moustache'). Well, Don Peppino was in the pulpit explaining materialism in scornful terms.

'*Il Baffone* has a new five-year plan. He tells everyone to work hard and make sacrifices… when the plan is finished, you can have your cow, a mule, a new pair of shoes. We know what it means to work for a long time and sacrifice… for the family, to buy a cow, an ass, a saddle, shoes. What *il Baffone* doesn't tell you is what you will get if you don't see the end of the five-year plan…. I'll tell you, my dear friends. You will get absolutely nothing! Not even the laces for a pair of shoes! But the most damning pain of all for the Communist… is that there is no God for him! There is no God for

him while alive, and no God in the hereafter! What a life! No God… no hope… nothing!'

It was then that the lights went out. Cantalupo's electrical power was under the control of a family with whom Don Peppino had quarrelled. No one knows whether or not the power cut was intentional, nevertheless, the interior of the church was in darkness.

There was a moment of silence before the voice of Don Peppino was heard, sounding as if it came from Dante's hell. 'A warning! If you disagree with *il Baffone* and his five-year plan, he has someone who, without warning, will take the light from your eyes, eh!' Don Peppino was masterly.

★ ★ ★

CANTALUPO'S PATRON SAINT is St Anne, protectress of pregnant women. In the old days, pregnant women from near and far used to carry a candle to the church and, with a prayer, light it before her altar. Grandmother, as we know, left seven candles at the altar. But for the daughter born in America, there would have been eight candles.

The *festa* of St Anne was (as it is today) the event of the year. It brought people together and attracted visitors from surrounding villages, a number of women arriving in traditional costumes with kite-like head coverings. Before the *festa*, trucks arrived with a portable bandstand and illuminations. The illuminations, suspended in a series of arches that approached the piazza, created a carnival atmosphere as merchants from Naples set up their stalls with goods not to be found in the modest village shops. Religious articles, kitchen goods, spades, pack saddles, harnesses and liniments for man and mule were hawked by the merchants. There was a stall piled with narrow-rimmed automobile tyres from which sandals were fashioned, and next to a stall with bolts of cloth was another, modestly popular in its way, with buttons, thread, assorted combs, hair pins and

ornamental clasps. The ice-cream vendor had his tubs before the bandstand, where his stacks of cones contributed to its Baroque setting, and the travelling photographer was always to be found in an open space with his pictorial backgrounds.

* * *

AFTER THE CELEBRATION of Mass at midday, the statue of St Anne, covered with old-fashioned jewelry, lira notes and American dollars, is brought out of the church, borne by a quartet of men who between them have donated to the church as much as one hundred kilos of grain, in competitive bidding, for the privilege of carrying the statue.

The brass band leads the way, followed by the clergy, parishioners and visitors. The statue is carried through the village, passing balconies draped with coverlets, exposed for the blessing of St Anne.

Finally, the procession comes to a pause at a site where a display of fireworks takes place, before St Anne is restored to her niche, to await the evening procession and a second display of pyrotechnics.

In the evening, everyone gathers in the piazza to be entertained by a dancing troupe from Naples and by the band performing operatic scores, with the trumpets rendering the inevitable Triumphal March from *Aida*.

* * *

I NEVER WALKED the kilometer up to the village on the day of my arrival; not far from the bus stop was the house of my grandparents. I had a room containing a pair of sepia-toned portraits of my grandparents, a shotgun with a cartridge belt hanging on a wall peg, a huge wardrobe and a wash-stand with a porcelain basin. For many months it was my studio until I packed the easel away and began to hang negatives to dry in the wardrobe.

As for domestic needs, aunt Vincenza, reciter of proverbs, looked after them as she did for her family. She was the youngest of the seven daughters. Months before she was born, my grandparents, already with six daughters – six dowries required – so desired a son that they hoped to aid and abet the issue by naming who-was-to-be, Vincenzo. My aunt was referred to as Vincenzo for all the hidden months, and when she did show herself as the seventh daughter – seven dowries, etc – my grandparents consoled each other by changing the masculine 'Vincenzo' to the feminine 'Vincenza'. The next born was the long-desired son and at last the seven sisters had a brother. He was named Vincenzo.

Sitting outdoors in the shade of the house with a flask of wine at my side, it was with aunt Vincenza – forever knitting – that aspects of the Italian and the American way of life were discussed. Her summing-up of the American way of life had a prophetic conclusion: when the American stands before the Gates of Paradise he will be denied entry, because he has already lived in Paradise. The only travelling she ever did, except for the occasional visit to her sisters in nearby towns, was with a group that undertook a pilgrimage to the major shrines of Rome, Loretto, Assisi and Padua. Her observations of life away from Cantalupo, under the guidance of prayer, left her with the conviction that *tutto il mondo e un paese* (all the world is a village).

In the Italian village there exists the 'trinity': the priest, the lawyer and the doctor. The priest attends to the parish and keeps in touch with those who have emigrated to Brooklyn and Montana, Montreal and Thunder Bay, Sydney and Waroonga. And every year from those far away places, Don Peppino receives contributions for the *festa* of St Anne. The list of contributors to a recent *festa* contains forty-one families with the name Monaco from distant places.

For the lawyer emigration was the main activity, for there are few lawsuits in poor peasantry. He collected the necessary documents, accompanied his clients to the embassies in Rome and to the seaport in Naples if he was the agent for a steamship line.

The doctor was young, he had to be. When not required in the village, he mounted his scooter and made his visits to the parishes situated far from the piazza; country dirt tracks demanded agility and stamina. Emigration kept him busy too. His medical report of an applicant was a necessary document.

There was no cinema in Cantalupo and TV aerials were not to be seen – yet. Although the last bundle of newspapers had been delivered long before the morning bus reached Cantalupo, the village was infested, like every other village, with weekly magazines that told their episodes of love and romance in pictorial strips. Bought, exchanged and bartered for, the magazines – 'Our Love', 'Dreams', 'Our Romance' – formed an escape and the recreation for the female population between the ages of adolescence and young motherhood.

★ ★ ★

RECREATION for the young man was playing cards in the cafe and *bocce* (bowls) along the provincial road. If the young man was adventurous, relatives in the New World would exchange a postal introduction for a marriage of convenience. If the exchange of snapshots furthered an encouragement, a correspondence would begin, hopefully ending with the girl packing her bridal gown and making the voyage to Cantalupo. With the nuptials and honeymoon over, the bride would return to the New World and initiate the action that would permit her newly acquired husband to join her.

* * *

SO IT WAS... when aunt Vincenza knitted sweaters for her grandchildren. So it was... when you met a farmer on the road and were very likely to be greeted with *'Cristo regna'* ('Christ reigns'). And the conversations you overheard dealt with the departure of a husband, brother or son for America; the curse of unemployment; the lack of rain; the failure of hens to lay eggs.

One day, a newly married couple passed the house walking hand in hand. Without a pause in her knitting, aunt Vincenza recited: *'Prim'anno, mano a mano/ Second'anno, cullo a cullo/ Terz'anno, calcio a cullo!'* ('First year, hand in hand/Second year, ass to ass/Third year, kick in the ass!')

The groom was due to emigrate, she went on to say, and was taking his bride to Naples before his departure. While in Naples, it would be prudent of them not to walk hand-in-hand but to keep their hands on their purses.

Several men from Naples, she recounted, used to come here during the hunting season and lodge with us, and they always advised, dress like a beggar if you visit Naples, keep your eyes open and your money in your shoe. One of the gentlemen, a railroad official at the main station, would leave his office whenever a foreign train was due to arrive, to wait for it at the platform, with porters, guides, the police, and always, an old, old man with a sign hanging round his neck, with the words 'Ceramics for Sale' on it. This old man has a suitcase as old as he is, filled with broken pieces of ceramics, and at his side are his two partners waiting with him for the train. Oh, the scoundrels! You will see how clever the Neopolitans are.

Now, when the train comes to a stop and hundreds of tourists are getting off it – our friend the railroad official told us – the old man starts walking along the platform with the suitcase on his shoulder and shouting, 'Ceramics-ceramics-ceramics'. What happens? The old man drops the suitcase. It breaks open and the ceramics shatter into a hundred bits at his feet. The old man then drops to his knees, takes off his hat and, beating his chest, begins to wail, 'Poor me! Poor me! Poor, poor me!'

What happens then? While the tourists stand there with their mouths open, staring at the wretched old man, one of his partners goes to him, pats him on the shoulder, says 'Poor old man', and puts money into his hat. The other partner pushes his way through

the crowd of tourists, goes to the old man and, shaking his head, puts money into his hat too. Dear nephew, one tourist, feeling pity, does the same thing, and as the old man continues to wail another tourist gives, and another, and another. The railroad official? He has a coffee at the bar and goes back to his office – the old man causes no harm with his suitcase of junk. Think of it, Cantalupo was part of the Kingdom of Naples; thank God, that was a long time ago.

* * *

ANOTHER DAY, my aunt put her knitting down. A young woman, she informed me, who worked the strip of land near the bombed bridge, had asked her if I would take a photograph of her baby, born a few days after her husband had emigrated. A long time would pass before her husband would be able to send the passage money for her to join him, and he wanted so much to have a picture of the baby.

I arrived with my camera while the young mother was breast-feeding the baby at her parent's home. The instant she saw me, she raised her kerchief to cover her hair and continued to feed her baby. After I took the photograph, her father offered me a glass of wine and remarked, with a sigh, that there was not to be a picture of the baby in the nude. Assuming that the baby had a deformity of some sort, I said nothing, but later I related what he had said to aunt Vincenza.

The wedding toast to the bride and groom, she explained, is '*Figli maschi*!' ('Sons!') The birth of a son is so desirable and joyous an event that when it takes place, the first picture is always a nude. The birth of a girl is another song: in time, a strict watch over her will be necessary and the dowry will have to be found. There were women, she added, who, after giving birth to a son, returned joyfully back to their work in the field in a day or two, at the most. As for the birth of a daughter… the woman would remain in bed with complaints for a week!

It was soon after that I was asked to photograph a child who had just recovered from a serious illness. The photograph was to reassure the father in Canada that all was well. I wanted to photograph mother and child together but she was too shy. It was the grandmother who posed with the child – wearing a cowl and knotted waist-cord – in her arms.

As for the cowl and cord, during the child's illness the mother, fearing for its life, prayed to St Francis and, as a token of gratitude, the child was to be dressed as a Franciscan friar for a year.

They say that a witch causes children to become ill, revealed aunt Vincenza. Now, if the mother were to stand a broom at the door before putting her child to bed, the witch would not molest the child. That is what they say....

The witch would take the broom and fly off?

You may laugh but there are mothers who do stand a broom at the door. They say that before the witch can enter the bedroom and cast a spell over the baby she has to count each bristle of the broom. If the witch has not counted all the bristles before sunrise, she must flee... the sun has power over the witch.

Witches and spells.... There was the evil eye too. An old man came by, raised his hat and, in conversation, remarked how lucky I was to be an American, living in the land of riches. When the old man left, aunt Vincenza said, 'If I believed in the evil eye, I would trace the sign of the Cross on your forehead.'

Why?

'To protect you from the evil eye. The old man gave you the evil eye because he did not say "God bless you" when he complimented you on being lucky. And did you see how his eyebrows met over his nose? It is said, beware of the man or woman with eyebrows that join when they pay you a compliment for your good fortune or your beauty, and don't say "God bless you". You are laughing, dear nephew? Well it is what people in these parts believe.'

* * *

TIME WENT BY, and I became regarded as the 'official' photographer of the hamlet. Invited, I photographed scores of mother-and-children portraits; babies in their baptismal dress; the mother in grief, bent over her dead child; the pause along the seashore during a pilgrimage. Whereas, uninvited, the furious grandmother drew her grandchild away from the camera: '*No! No! Si tolga l'anima!*' ('No! No! You will take away her soul!')

In return for the photographs, wine, salami and olive oil were left for me with aunt Vincenza, who once inquired, while preparing a salad, if Don Peppino's prayers to St Catherine (patroness of the arts) were worth as much as a spoon's measure of olive oil.

* * *

IN THE PHOTOGRAPH in which the grandmother holds the child dressed in cowl and waist-cord, the calendar on the wall is dated 1953. I wonder if the child is listed as a contributor to the *festa* of St Anne. Could he be Augustino Bernadi of Montreal? Or Antonio Rico of Toronto? Has the baby girl, whose picture I did not take in the nude, become Anna Gale of Cleveland? Did the girl herding the sheep and black goat (who ignored my greeting) become Lisa Husjake, and live in Newark? And the pensive blue-eyed boy with his smiling mother, could he be Francesco Di Re, in Canberra?

I know that the man standing in the wheat field, with jug raised for a drink, never left Cantalupo. The two ladies in the shallow surf – I knew them well. They were my aunts, two of the seven daughters.

* * *

CANTALUPO. The tall poplars have been removed but the klaxon sounds of the Rome bus are still heard. A new bridge has replaced the one that was bombed, and every foot of the road up to the village has been paved. The lawyer has closed his studio and left the piazza – emigration is over – and the unemployed now leave for Milan and Turin. And on the day of the *festa*, when Mass is celebrated, the congregation listening to Don Peppino is joined by a score of Cantalupesi from faraway places, who have returned to the old country for a visit.

★ ★ ★

AUNT VINCENZA. She travels to New Jersey, stays awhile with her son, and she travels to Buenos Aires, stays awhile with her daughter but, God bless her, she always returns for the *festa*.

★ ★ ★

POSTSCRIPT

Aunt Vincenza, last of the seven daughters, reciter of proverbs, has passed away. She was ninety-four years old. Don Peppino told me that, in the end, she had become *un po inquieta* (a little restless), she worried that God had forgotten her.

A year later, Don Peppino passed away. Before the new priest arrived in Cantalupo, I removed a row of photographs from the walls of the vestry, photographs taken of street shrines found in Naples.

Don Peppino loved the street shrines. 'Look at those shrines of God', he said one day. 'They are in the alleys of Naples, eh. Those alleys, a Christian can traverse only with the protection of St Christopher and a guardian angel!' Then, softly in voice, as if talking to himself, continued, 'But St Bruno used to say, "Goodness is everywhere".' And turning to me, added, 'He is… isn't He?'

Fifty years have gone by in Cantalupo; with them aunt Vincenza, the village priest and those who left for the New World. A way of life has disappeared. A few traces of that life can be seen in these photographs and, with them, are the eight images of the Neopolitan shrines to God, which I removed from the walls of Don Peppino's vestry.

★ ★ ★

A Kaleidoscope of
BUTTERFLIES

A celebration of Britain's 59 species

Jonathan Bradley

Photographs by Yealand Kalfayan ARPS

MERLIN UNWIN BOOKS

For Harriet

First published in Great Britain by Merlin Unwin Books Ltd, 2020

Text © Jonathan Bradley 2020
Photographs © Yealand Kalfayan 2020 (see also credits on page 185)

Merlin Unwin Books Ltd
Palmers House
7 Corve Street
Ludlow
Shropshire SY8 1DB
U.K.

www.merlinunwin.co.uk

The author asserts his moral right to be identified with this work.

ISBN 978-1-910723-99-9

Designed by Jo Dovey
Printed by DZS Grafik, Slovenia

Contents

Foreword

I am delighted to be contributing the foreword to this wonderful book written by Jonathan Bradley, a member of Butterfly Conservation (BC), especially as a donation to BC will be made from sales of the book. It is illustrated with beautiful photographs, many of them taken by another BC member, Yealand Kalfayan. BC's vision is for a world where butterflies and moths thrive and can be enjoyed by everyone, forever. Our mission focuses on achieving four main aims: to recover threatened butterflies and moths, increase numbers of widespread species, inspire people to understand and deliver species conservation, and promote international conservation action. These aims encompass our practical conservation work, research, management of reserves, raising awareness and much more.

The impact BC has had since 1968 has been huge. We now have over 40,000 members, 220,000 days of volunteer effort per year, over 100,000 citizen scientists taking part in the Big Butterfly Count and 92 members of staff, all implementing BC's conservation work on the ground and providing the vital data records we need to monitor the state of our butterflies and moths. In order for BC to continue its fantastic work for decades to come we need to strengthen our resilience for the future by expanding our research, connecting people to nature and green spaces, growing and supporting volunteers, and securing sufficient funding for priority species and landscape scale conservation work.

It is sobering to realise that several of the butterflies featured in the book are rare, threatened or endangered. For instance, the High Brown Fritillary has been highlighted by BC as Britain's most threatened butterfly; the species has seen a 79% decline in distribution since the 1970s. Yet, in the words of Jonathan's poem, it has been able 'even so to survive against the odds'. The future of several other butterflies in this book is very precarious. We might all hope that, like the Clouded Yellow in its poem, all our butterflies could have 'no care but to rise up and fly' rather than be 'condemned to perish for an unknown sin', as in the Mountain Ringlet poem.

I hope that *A Kaleidoscope of Butterflies* will open the eyes and hearts of the British public to the beauty and the plight of the butterflies that all of us at BC so passionately wish to conserve.

Julie Williams
Chief Executive of Butterfly Conservation
January 2020

Preface

This is a kaleidoscopic display in words and pictures of fifty-nine species of butterfly that occur naturally in Great Britain, as well as some rare visitors and a few of the remarkable people who have loved them. Each of the butterflies has a brief story and my own original poem. They have flown into my life many times, often unexpectedly, and usually in beautiful places, so they bring happy memories. Each one also is pictured in stunning photographs, most of which were taken by my friend and fellow butterfly lover, Yealand Kalfayan, an Associate of the Royal Photographic Society.

I should stress that I am not a scientist and I do not claim to be an 'expert'. I do love butterflies and the natural environment in which we all live, and this passion led me to write this book. The poems are in various different poetic forms, in some cases just for the fun of trying something different. As a result, some of the poems follow strict patterns of metre and rhyme, and others are frankly light-hearted and trifling. I hope that purists will not be offended.

The names of butterflies are almost as colourful as their wings in most languages, and each of them has a scientific name from the Linnaean system written in the Latin style. Many of them are derived from ancient mythologies, usually Greek or Roman, but others are obscure in origin. Where the name seems to have an identifiable meaning I have written something about it. These names are poetic, and butterflies are part of the poetry of nature. They also matter greatly for the future health of our world. From time to time scientists change the scientific names, and so to avoid confusion I have used the names that appear in *The Millennium Atlas of Butterflies in Britain and Ireland*, by Jim Asher et al, Oxford University Press, 2001.

My children introduced me to butterflies. I found that trying to stalk and spot birds with noisy toddlers was very frustrating, and butterflies were less scared of us, so we searched for them instead. They are so colourful, and live in such beautiful places, that we were all captivated. Butterflies soon became a passion. Now my children themselves have children, and these grandchildren will go looking for butterflies. I hope that enough butterflies will be saved from decline or extinction that Isla, Jago, Rebekah, Merryn, Leila, Astrid and Leo can each look forward to a long lifetime of butterfly watching. If so, their lives will be lit with the pleasure of visiting beautiful places to observe some of the most remarkable creatures of the natural world.

I soon realised that without friendly habitats, butterflies could not flourish, and that they represent a highly sensitive barometer of the natural world. Pollution, pesticides, reckless building development, loss of green spaces, and reduction of plant diversity – all result in the death or even extinction of butterflies. A world without butterflies would, in the end, be a world without people.

There must be something very special about these small, fragile, short-lived creatures that could have united in their love for them such diverse people as a Bulgarian king, a French composer, a Russian novelist, the first female Fellow of the Royal Entomological Society and many others. Several of them are featured here.

This book is not only about butterflies but also about people. We depend on each other. Though they may not be aware of it, butterflies give us enormous pleasure, and in my case the inspiration to write about them.

Adonis Blue
Polyommatus bellargus

Adonis was a beautiful youth in Greek mythology, and the name suits a butterfly whose male wears one of the most stunning colours of any British butterfly. The male is a brilliant iridescent blue, variously described as azure, sky blue or turquoise. This is impossible to describe adequately in words, and has to be seen to be believed. Remarkably, much of this colour is generated by light refraction rather than as a result of pigmentation in the wings. The females are brown. The poem recounts some of the story in the myth, and especially Adonis's unfortunate need to choose between two divine women, one of whom, feeling rejected, arranges for him to be killed by a wild boar. But he was not forgotten, as the poem tells us.

Adonis Blue male displaying his brilliant azure colouring.

Adonis Blue, underside. The brown colour helps to camouflage it when resting on stony ground or rocky surfaces.

The first part of the scientific name roughly means 'many-eyed', referring to the many-coloured spots underneath its wings. *Bellargus* in Latin means 'beautiful Argus'. We meet Argus in his many guises elsewhere, and a fuller story appears in the section about the Peacock butterfly. As divorce on Mount Olympus was not straightforward, Zeus's wife Hera revenged herself on her unfaithful husband by transplanting the eyes of Argus to the tail of a peacock. This may seem a curious form of vengeance, but Argus was Zeus's agent in an important mission and he was blinded in the process. The Adonis Blue has small eye-spots on the underside of its wings. By no means all of the possible identities of Argus – many-eyed monster guard of an errant heifer, shipbuilder, dog or local newspaper – are necessarily beautiful, but the butterfly certainly is.

I have not often seen this butterfly, but it always delights. My sightings have been mainly on Dorset and Wiltshire downland, as its two broods occur in this country only in southern England during May/June and August/September. The larvae feed on horseshoe vetch, and then overwinter before pupating in the spring. They often have ants as personal attendants. The ants love the sweet secretions given off by the larvae, and sometimes bury larvae at night to protect them from predators.

.

Adonis Blue

Lovely Adonis had to choose
between the goddess of pleasure and love
and the queen of the underworld;
was it any surprise that he chose love?

After she found him near to death
Aphrodite mingled nectar with his blood,
and made of it a running stream;
every Levantine spring
his river flows blood-red.
By the bank his short-lived flower, Anemone,
evaporates in puffs of breeze.

Adonis Blues, his many souls,
released from Olympian jealousy,
are reborn in nature on the Wiltshire Downs
in brilliant turquoise incarnations:
the near-divine in frailest form
too small to be attacked
by wild boar that killed
their forebear demi-god.

Rothschilds:
Walter (1868-1937)
and Miriam (1908-2005)

These two members of the same famous Jewish banking family were uncle and niece, and both were keen lovers of butterflies, and in their different ways very distinguished. Miriam wrote an affectionate biography of her uncle, details of which are at the end of this book.

Walter was the second baron Rothschild, and his brother Charles was Miriam's father. Among many other claims to fame he was an eccentric lepidopterist and nature-lover. On one occasion he drove to Buckingham Palace in a carriage drawn by zebras, and on another occasion was photographed riding on a giant tortoise in his garden.

When younger he travelled widely in search of biological specimens, sometimes on butterfly-netting expeditions in the company of 'Foxy' Ferdinand, King of Bulgaria and father of King Boris III who appears elsewhere in this book. He also sent members of staff and of his own family on similar missions. Butterfly hunting usually involves plenty of travel. In 1892 he opened a private museum at Tring in Hertfordshire. It housed an enormous natural history collection, including, it is said, over two million butterflies. Some of these were species named after him.

His niece Miriam was no less remarkable, as she had little formal early schooling but she still became a renowned natural scientist and author, with a special interest in butterflies and eventually a Dame Commander of the Most Excellent Order of the British Empire (DBE). She was honoured with honorary doctorates but did not take one herself. Her scientific achievements were so highly regarded that even the eminent, but famously misogynistic, Oxford biologist and butterfly expert E. B. Ford was prepared to befriend her.

For those, like the author of this book, who are as captivated by the beauty and mystery of butterflies as by the sober science of their biology, Miriam Rothschild's book *Butterfly Cooing Like A Dove* is delightful to read. It is a rich anthology of butterfly (and dove) miscellany, in which she has collected pictures, stories, legends, and quotations from diverse writers such as Nabokov and Proust, all about butterflies. It is very clear that she was a true butterfly enthusiast.

.

Black Hairstreak
Satyrium pruni

In Britain this rare butterfly occurs only in parts of the Midlands, and is one of a family of Hairstreaks. It would be even more rare without the work of Walter Rothschild, featured here in a mini-biography. He is said to have arranged for large numbers of Black Hairstreaks to be released in the areas where they still now occur. To see some you will need to visit woodlands between Oxford and Peterborough during its single flight period, which is generally mid-June to mid-July. Even then you may find them difficult to spot.

The scientific name literally means either a herbal drink made from Satyrion (ragwort) and plums, acting as an aphrodisiac if it does not kill you, or a Satyr in trees of the Prunus tree genus, of which Blackthorn is a member. Blackthorn is the favoured food plant of the larvae of this butterfly. The male and female look very alike, and their eggs overwinter and hatch in the spring.

The English name refers to the 'Black' member of the Hairstreak family. In fact this one is more buff-brown with orange markings, as seen in the photograph. Hairstreaks are so called because they tend to have transverse streaks on the under-surface of the wings and delicate, hair-like tails on their hindwings.

At the time of writing I still have not seen a living Black Hairstreak insect, although I have sometimes spotted a human being with the kind of streaked hair described in this poem. A condition known as poliosis can cause coloured hair to have a streak of white. Occasionally the reverse is seen, with a dark streak in the white, as possessed by the late playwright, Samuel Beckett.

Black Hairstreak underside.
The orange and black markings
on the hindwings may fool a
predator to attack the rear rather
than the head.

Black Hairstreak

My hair was blond with a streak of black.

Sometimes in the playground they were cruel;
while boys were busy peeing over walls
the girls were staring at my curls,
blond with a black streak.
'Cindy's a freak –
she kissed the devil.'

But later, older, I stood out.
Boys looked, and sometimes stroked
to see if it felt different;
it didn't, but I did.
'Is it dyed?' I could have died.

Later still, the blond turned grey
but black stayed black
and I felt special,
and like the Black Hairstreak butterfly
rare and beautiful.

Brimstone
Gonepteryx rhamni

This is the original 'butterfly', mentioned in the fourteenth century Nun's Priest's Prologue of the *Canterbury Tales* by Geoffrey Chaucer:

> *'Your tale annoys the entire company;*
> *Such talking is not worth a butterfly;*
> *For in it is no sport nor any game.'*

It is a shame that Chaucer does not rate highly the importance of a butterfly, but he gives us proof of the use of the word in his time.

It is so called because the male is a butter-coloured shade of yellow. It is thought that the word 'butterfly' may have gained a generic meaning because the Brimstone is often one of the first butterflies to be seen on the wing in spring. As it happens, yellow is also the colour of brimstone, an archaic word for sulphur, as in 'fire and brimstone'. The females are greenish-white colour.

The Brimstone gives us a cheerful reminder on a bright day in late February or March that spring really is on the way, that we should cheer up after winter gloom, and that we should look forward to a new butterfly season. It seems to turn up all over the place, at least in England, and its spontaneous appearance is one of its attractions. It is one of the few British butterflies to overwinter as an adult, and is therefore one of the longest lived.

Gonepteryx rhamni is a descriptive name. The first part of the name is Latin for 'angular wing', the wings of Brimstone butterflies indeed being angular. The second part refers to Buckthorn, the favoured food plant of Brimstone larvae.

My poem imagines the life cycle of an adult Brimstone, as it first emerges from its chrysalis and then flies off in the sunshine.

A post-hibernation leaf-like male Brimstone, its wings slightly worn, rests on apple blossom.

Brimstone

At the first glimmer I was aware,
even before the wrench
from tight cocoon
to daylight spring
in a bright eruption of light,
conscious but unknowing
and without speech.
There were urgencies, but which first?

I was Brimstone without fire
but nectar from the dandelion
    felt fiery inside.
        I brought news of the
            fresh season and I was
               Chaucer's butter fly.

My wings stretched taut,
my legs stood straight,
then terror as shadow blocked the sun:
a great winged beast
snapped at my wing;
no scream of flight: I had no voice
but then was not my end
there were flowers to find
my own sulphur blooms
like me, fruit of the earth.

I gorged on celandine, crowfoot, clover,
always in peril from ravenous beaks.
I knew not what I was.
When on the brim
I found my other Brimstone and
we were joined on buckthorn.
Among the nursery leaves
she laid her eggs.

I sunned myself flat
on a Habsburg wall,
barely visible but nearly safe;
that night was cold,
but I felt nothing.

Brown Argus
Aricia agestis

If it is possible for any brown colour to look brilliant then that is the colour of both sexes of this butterfly. A little confusingly it is a member of the Lycaenid family of butterflies, many of which are blue, but this one is a very fine dark chocolate shade (see page 12). I have often seen Brown Arguses in early or late summer in wild grassy places such as the Iron Age hillfort at Barbury Castle in Wiltshire.

It has May/June and July/September broods, and overwinters as a larva, pupating in the spring, with help from ants.

The scientific name *Aricia* probably comes from Ariccia, a town near Rome, where there was a temple of Diana. She was a Roman goddess of hunting, the moon, wild animals and woodland, as well as the virgin goddess of childbirth and women. Like many other deities of the ancient world she had to be adept at multi-tasking. *Agestis* has an unclear origin and has no apparent meaning. It may be an erroneous derivation from the Latin 'ager', meaning meadow.

My poem refers to some of the many Arguses that have appeared in history and literature. The introduction to the Peacock butterfly section explains more about them.

Brown Argus, underside. Superficially similar to the female Common Blue, but the wing spots are slightly different.

Brown Argus upperside, sunbathing and displaying. There's no blue at the base of its wings.

Opposite page: Brown Argus underwin probably roostin

Brown Argus

Argus history is rich,
as long as the insect is small.

Argus Panoptes, the ancient giant
with a hundred eyes never all asleep,
no longer jealously guards
the heifer-nymph, Io the goddess.

Argus of the Argo, builder of Jason's ship,
sailed with his master in search of the fleece,
then watched him bewitched by Medea
and scoured caves for dragons' teeth;
we know not if he witnessed
the rotting timbers from his Argo hulk
cut short Jason's lonely disillusion.

Argus, Odysseus's favourite dog,
as faithful as Penelope,
knew the scent of the King of Ithaca
on his return after twenty years,
even before his wife.

The Argus of Brighton
surveys and purveys
small town stories, gossip history.

The Brown Argus butterfly
carries news of natural living history:
of downland chalk and nectar flowers
of bulldozers, lost meadows,
supermarket car parks.

The same lunule-spotted wings
could have settled on the giant's eyelid,
Jason's wedding flowers,
Odysseus's battered cuirass,
or Brighton classified ads,
just as they now lie defiant
on a concrete path.

Brown Hairstreak

Thecla betulae

Thecla was a saint of the early Christian Church, much revered by the Byzantine Greeks. According to legend, despite several attempts on her virginity she remained celibate during a long life, and was saved from martyrdom several times. The onset of a storm rescued her from being burnt at the stake, and when thrown in an arena with wild animals she survived because the females refused to eat her. There is no obvious reason why her name should have been chosen for a very elusive small brown and orange butterfly. *Betulae* means 'of birch trees', a name possibly assigned under the mistaken impression that the larval food plant of the butterfly is birch, when in fact it is blackthorn.

Hairstreaks are so called because they tend to have transverse streaks on the under-surface of the wings and delicate, hair-like tails on their hindwings.

Brown Hairstreaks are notoriously difficult to find because they are mainly restricted to the south of Wales and England and the adults spend much of their life at the tops of trees. In parts of Devon and Somerset they are not uncommon but still elusive, and you need to be very patient to spot one. The best chance is to catch a glimpse when they have condescended to come down from the canopy to feed on bramble flowers. The males are darker in colour than females, which can look golden and have a bright orange patch on their upper wings. Females also have longer tails. There is one brood and the butterfly overwinters as an egg.

I have a soft spot for all five of our native Hairstreaks precisely because they all tend to be rather shy, but also because of the tails that they have at the end of their hindwings which make them look as though they have dressed for an outing.

**Opposite: A female Brown
Hairstreak warms herself on a leaf.
She has large orange patches
on the forewings.**

Brown Hairstreak

This elusive insect makes us think:
of the one pale pebble on a slate-grey beach,
a shining ivy leaf on a creeper cascade,
the face on a train that catches the eye,
a small bedraggled daisy given by a child,
the first sparrow on the morning bird-table,
a glass of iced water in the desert,
freshly dug earth for the potato patch,
scent of an unseen pine in the summer woods,
one empty seat in a crowded concert hall,
the terraced house where Turner lived,
night stars appearing when clouds blow by.

But how should we describe the Thecla Betulae?
Brown. Small. Dull. Rare.
It is no martyred virgin,
and does not feed on birch.

Si non videbo, etiamtunc cogitabo.*

* 'If I never see it, I shall still picture it in my mind's eye.'

Above: Underside of the Brown Hairstreak. Note the tails at the back of the wing.

Camberwell Beauty
Nymphalis antiopa

Although rarely seen in the British Isles, the Camberwell Beauty is so striking in appearance that it has gained several names over the centuries, and is a very welcome visitor from Scandinavia. Only the adult is ever seen here, and it rarely overwinters. The eighteenth-century entomologist and engraver Moses Harris, in his book of 1766, *The Aurelian*, named this butterfly 'the Grand Surprise', no doubt because he saw it as memorable but rare. It had first been recorded eighteen years earlier, in 1748, at Camberwell in south London, which was then a rural parish. It was found again there in 1793 and gained another name, Camberwell Beauty. It would be unlikely to occur there now because urban London has spread.

A female Camberwell Beauty (underside) feeds on fermenting sap.

A Camberwell Beauty nectaring on a thistle seed head.

It has borne at least three further names in English: Willow Beauty, White Petticoat, and, in America, the more sombre name of Mourning Cloak. The German name is Trauermantel, meaning the same, and it is thought likely that the name came via German immigrant settlers to America. Its brownish-maroon and lemon colouring shows up well in Yealand's photograph.

The first part of the scientific Latin name, *Nymphalis*, is from ancient Greek nympha. Nymphs were lesser deities believed to be found near streams and in forests, and in mythology often experienced the mixed blessing of being carried off by lustful gods. *Antiopa* was one such. Having borne Zeus two sons, she then married Lycus, king of Thebes, who later ran off with another woman. She was probably better off without him. By contrast, the butterfly that bears these names is quite a free spirit and capable of flying right over the North Sea.

My poem refers to three of the English names, but my favourite is Grand Surprise, as will be clear from the last line.

Camberwell Beauty

Does this beauty really mourn?
Perhaps the passage of youth?
The insistence of small nuisances?
Over-indulgence on honeyed nectar?
Fading memories of Camberwell?
She is too handsome
to be mourning her own reflection.
She may not be mourning at all,
rejoicing in her own deep maroon
edged with sunshine.
She delights by bursting
unexpected into a late summer party,
a welcome gate-crasher
with velvet colours
swept from Swedish forests.
She is far from her birthplace, but happy,
a homeless wanderer greeted
in English meadows as a treasured guest.
Her cloak may be tenebrous but she does not weep
because she has never seen Camberwell.
She is the Grand Surprise.

Chalkhill Blue

Polyommatus coridon

This is a downland butterfly, and reminds me of summer days in southern England with skylarks singing overhead. It has one generation that flies in July and August, and their eggs hatch in the spring when the larvae begin feeding on their sole food plant, horseshoe vetch. The males are a lovely pale blue, and the females brown.

The first part of the scientific name roughly means 'many-eyed', referring to the many-coloured spots underneath its wings, and *Coridon* was a name often given to shepherds in classical literature. It was in particular the name of a pederastic shepherd who loved a boy called Alexis in Virgil's *Eclogues*. The name is derived from a Greek word for lark, suggesting a coincidental association with the skylarks that I mentioned above.

The English name refers to one of the favoured habitats of the butterfly, chalk grassland, although the butterfly is also happy on the kind of limestone downland found at Draycott Sleights in Somerset. There is a nature reserve there with superb views over the Somerset Levels and Severn Estuary. In the summer Chalkhill Blues fly over the wild flowers while grasshoppers jump as you walk.

A male Chalkhill Blue displaying (showing off!).

The undersides of two male Chalkhill Blues.

Chalkhill Blue

Under the midnight moon,
cold and cruel,
you held me through my winter night
as I mourned an impossible life,
until the cracked window steamed
right across from side to side.

Now we lie and linger
on the blue-green downs
stretching on the horse-shoe vetch;
the skylarks sing
church bells ring
and all around us
Chalkhill Blues abounding,
my mind at rest, at one with yours,
your fingers and mine entwined.

A female Chalkhill Blue roosting.
Her brown colour helps in avoiding
detection.

Chequered Skipper

Carterocephalus palaemon

As the poem describes, it has in recent times been possible to see the Chequered Skipper only in parts of Scotland and north-east England. It has one generation a year and the larvae feed on grasses and then overwinter in that state.

Skipper butterflies probably gained their name from their energetic flight that gives the impression that they are skipping from flower to flower. They have broad heads in relation to the rest of their bodies. Indeed, the Dutch call them Dikkop vlinder, or 'broad-headed butterfly', and the first part of the scientific Latin name, *Carterocephalus*, means 'strong head'. *Palaemon*, a god of seafarers and harbours, had a somewhat difficult start in life when his mother, after being scared by the goddess Hera, jumped from cliffs into the sea with him in her arms. They were both transformed into sea gods, and Palaemon is often depicted in ancient mosaics as either a dolphin-riding boy or a fish-tailed child. This is a somewhat random naming for a butterfly that has no direct connection with the sea.

The English name Chequered Skipper is simply descriptive – see the picture. Yealand's photograph has captured a healthy specimen feeding on cranesbill.

In 2018 Butterfly Conservation arranged for the release of adult Chequered Skipper butterflies at a secret location in Rockingham Forest, Northamptonshire, where they had flown in the

The Chequered Skipper's larval foodplant is the purple moor-grass of north-west Scotland

A Chequered Skipper warming itself on a rocky surface. Note the broad head.

Chequered Skipper

To see a Chequered Skipper
you must search the Scottish glens
when wind and sun do not scowl –
and even then they're hard to spot.

If you're lucky you will find one
even if you cannot hear or smell,
but what if you are blind?

The whispering hint
of Skipper wings in flight
is far too slight for human ears,
and mountain scents will overwhelm
for human nose a Skipper pheromone.

It is a visual creature,
alive in your sight, but otherwise a figment;
and if you cannot hear or smell or see,
and never hear or smell or see,
there is the very smallest chance
if you wait still as a stone
in the bracken
the purple moor grass may brush your cheek
and maybe, maybe
a breath, a chance of air
as Skipper wings glance by,
a sense of gold and chocolate brown –
an aural vision, an answered prayer.

past. It was hoped that these butterflies would mate and create a new English population of Chequered Skippers in the forest.

At the time of writing in 2019 adults had emerged successfully and were flying about and mating. There is hope that a sustainable colony will be re-established.

A mating pair of Chequered Skippers on a stem of broom.

Clouded Yellow

Colias croceus

The Clouded Yellow is a migrant visitor to this country in variable numbers. In favourable conditions large numbers may arrive, and butterfly enthusiasts refer to such events as a 'Clouded Yellow year', notably in 1877, 1947, 1983, 1992, 1994, 1996 and 2000. This wonderful happening is what I imagine in my poem.

When this occurs, Clouded Yellows can be seen rather randomly in many parts of the country, but especially in the south. A few years ago I was astonished to find dozens of them feeding on summer flowers on the grassy banks above Boscastle harbour in Cornwall. At first, from a distance, I thought they might be Brimstones, but as I approached I could see they were something much more unusual for this country. This brought on the 'lepidopterist thrill' that can still tingle after many years of butterfly watching. Most of the holiday makers who had struggled from the car park as far as the harbour with the grassy bank did not seem to have noticed the exceptional insect visitors all around them, and it struck me how much they were missing. This was all the more reason for writing this book.

It was long thought that Clouded Yellows could not overwinter in this

Clouded Yellow

When the nectar fields wilt in the sun
of the southernmost pastures of France
and in Spain it's too hot to be fun,
there's a stir from Cádiz to the Rance.

Clouded Yellows are up in the air,
rising out of the clover baked dry,
energetic with saffronesque flair
and no care but to rise up and fly.

Under unclouded skies they depart,
guided only by ancestral drive,
a display of bold kinetic art,
risking death in the need to survive.

Over forests and cliffs, sandy bays,
they migrate and, descending, appear
as confetti on their mating days
for an English Clouded Yellow year.

A female Clouded Yellow feeding on ragwort.
See the long, curled proboscis.

country, but there have been more recent records of survival through the winter, possibly because of the warming climate. In good years in Britain it can have several broods, with the larvae feeding mainly on clover. Females are slightly larger than males, with different wing borders.

There are two other types of this butterfly that can be seen in the UK, the Pale Clouded Yellow and Berger's Clouded Yellow, though much less frequently than their near-namesake. As the Pale Clouded Yellow is very difficult to tell apart from the Clouded Yellow I somewhat arbitrarily felt that it did not yet deserve its own poem. Maybe someday I shall tackle it, but the Berger's does appear later in the book. On the other hand, if Dr Maurice Fontaine is to be believed, Berger does not deserve the credit because Dr Fontaine found the new butterfly first and Berger pinched his discovery. The world of lepidopterology can be very ruthless as well as eccentric.

It is not clear why the word 'clouded' is included in its English name, because it loves bright sunshine, like all butterflies. It may have arisen because the upper wing of the Clouded Yellow has grey edges, making them look a little overcast.

The scientific name, *Colias croceus,* is just as complicated. Aphrodite *Colias* was one of the personas of Aphrodite, goddess of love, and in that guise she was worshipped in a temple near Athens. She also makes an appearance in the play *Lysistrata* by Aristophanes, which tells of the attempt by ancient Greek women to bring about peace by denying the pleasures of the bedroom to their warrior husbands until they ceased fighting. This is not a practice followed by Clouded Yellow butterflies, as is shown by their capacity to multiply quickly.

Croceus is Latin for golden yellow, so this butterfly was clearly considered by those who named it to be very yellow.

A male Clouded Yellow resting after a feed. Note his greenish-yellow eye. Butterfly eye colours vary.

Comma
Polygonia c-album

This butterfly resembles a flying leaf, and has delightfully improbable wings. It tends to turn up unexpectedly, and sometimes you are not sure if you have really seen it, as it flies strongly and suddenly from flower to flower.

In the spring it can be seen almost anywhere in England and Wales after emerging from its hibernation.

There is then a complicated life cycle. Those butterflies that wake in March mate and produce a generation that appears in midsummer. Most of the offspring have dark undersides and go on to hibernate. However, some of this generation have lighter, brighter wings and are known as the form *hutchinsoni*. It is thought that some larvae that grow when days are lengthening tend

A Comma, showing its upperside, rests on some nectar-rich verbena flowers.

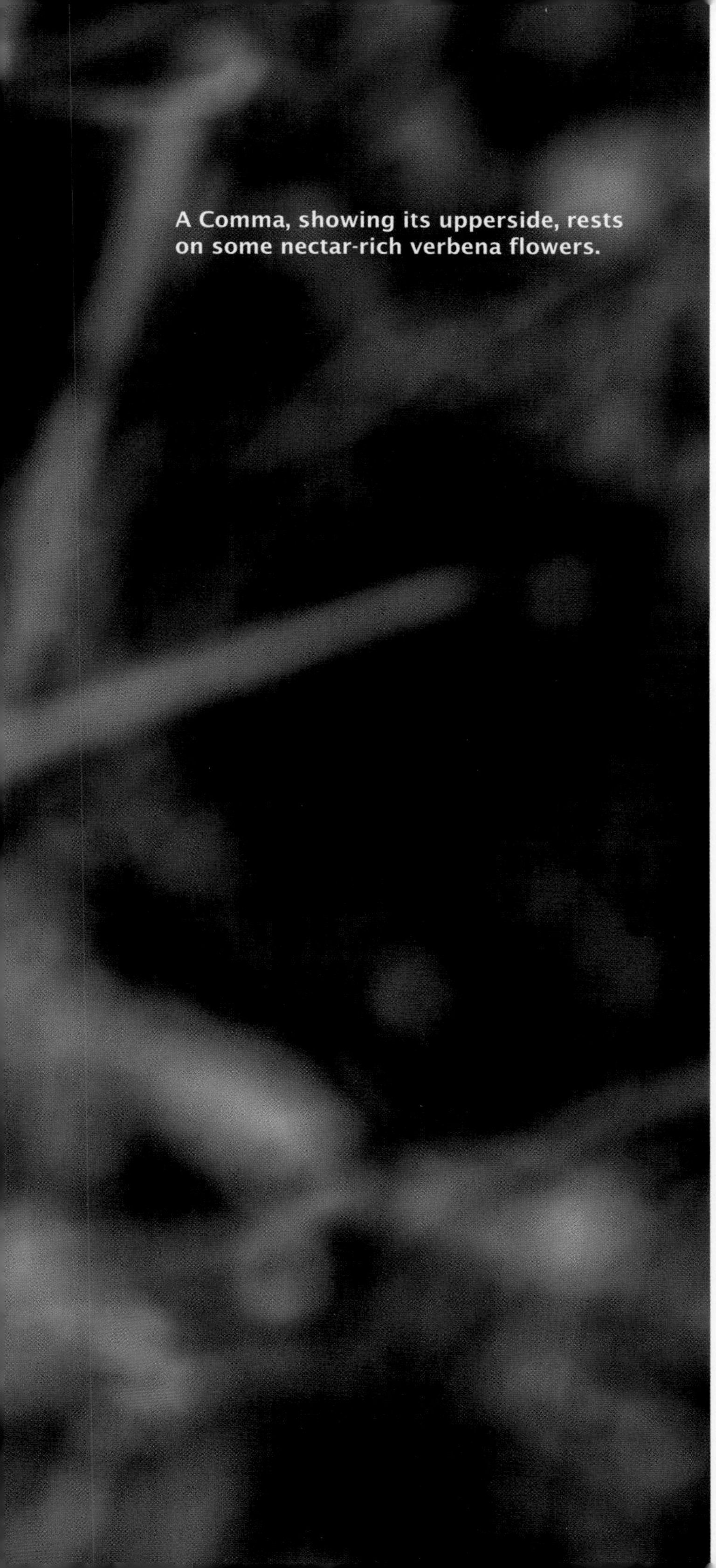

to develop into *hutchinsoni* adults, while those developing as days shorten will more likely be darker. You can read about the *hutchinsoni* variety on page 50 in the section about Eleanor Glanville. The larvae usually feed on nettles, but sometimes on hops, currants or willows.

The scientific name means 'many-sided shape with a white C'. Similarly, the English name refers to the comma-shaped white mark on the underside of the hindwing. In the circumstances the poem was almost bound to be about punctuation.

Comma

A natural pause;
I break my step to read
a leafy punctuation of my daydream –
live but impossible;

here is foliage escaping
in quotation marks;

the sentence for
this wordless being
for contravening
nature's grammar
is never to come to a stop,

Common Blue

Polyommatus icarus

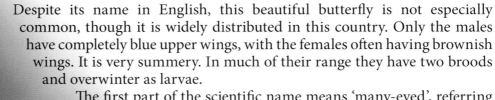

Despite its name in English, this beautiful butterfly is not especially common, though it is widely distributed in this country. Only the males have completely blue upper wings, with the females often having brownish wings. It is very summery. In much of their range they have two broods and overwinter as larvae.

The first part of the scientific name means 'many-eyed', referring to the many-coloured spots underneath its wings. The name *Polyommatus* is shared with its two much more rare relatives, the Adonis Blue and the Chalkhill Blue.

Icarus was the mythical Greek character imprisoned with his father Daedalus in the Labyrinth with the terrifying Minotaur. Daedalus made wings for himself and his son, stuck on with wax, to allow them to escape. Before they escaped, Daedalus warned Icarus not to fly too close to the sun, as the wax would melt, and the wings would fall off. Sadly, Icarus forgot the warning, and flew too close, so his wings came off and he drowned in the sea.

Strangles is a beach near Boscastle in north Cornwall. As you pick your way down a steep path towards the Atlantic you come upon a precipitous and wild undercliff. Some years ago most of the vegetation and wildlife were burnt in a brush fire. The wings of butterflies, like

The underside of a male Common Blue nectaring.

those of Icarus, would have melted quickly in the fire. Much to my joy, though, the wings of the Common Blue butterflies quite soon returned; hence this poem. The traditional folk-name that my mother taught me for bird's-foot trefoil, a main food plant for the larvae of the Common Blue, is 'eggs and bacon', because it often has both yellow and pinkish-red flowers.

These very attractive butterflies can be seen almost anywhere in the British Isles in the summer months, but especially in wild and unspoilt places.

Pair of Common Blues mating – male on the right, female on the left.

Common Blue

A Common Blue
resting on plantain.

Red and gold consumed Strangles,
tore away purple, green and ochre,
and bequeathed black.

Fire, the fool's life, rejoiced, ran wild
feasting to the death
on the mystic life of growing things.

Flames baked the adder in the stones;
burning embers seared the hands of ivy
where they clung to trees;
ash buried the thyme
and tormentil wilted in the blaze.

The wings of the Blue, when they lit,
made a minuscule spark
- Icarus burnt from below.

The land was charred,
cauterized, and carbonised
but still life hid in damp folds
slowly persisted in cracks and holes
without hope
abode and lived.

Sheltered and saved by a tussock of grass
the bird's-foot trefoil breathed
- eggs and bacon unfried;
and over the wastes flew the female Blue,
a healing patch of sky,
and laid her eggs
in the gold and red flowers.

So azure wings
will fly again next spring
across the cinders greening.

Dark Green Fritillary
Argynnis aglaja

Argynnis is one of the names for Aphrodite, the ancient Greek goddess of love and beauty. The name may have come from ancient Indian lore, and refers to the brilliance of the dawn. *Aglaea*, or Radiance, was one of the three Graces, wife of Hephaestus after he separated from Aphrodite. So, the scientific name for this butterfly refers to two different wives of Hephaestus, who was the Greek god of blacksmiths and volcanoes. These allusions seem quite fitting for such a large and splendid butterfly, striking, though not as a fulminating blacksmith might be.

The English name, like so many butterfly names, is misleading. The Dark Green Fritillary is mainly not green, but a russet orange-brown with black stripes above, and green and silver underneath. The name distinguishes it from other Fritillaries that do not have this patch of greenish hue. The female is slightly lighter coloured than the male.

The name Fritillary is derived from the Latin word '*fritillus*', meaning dice-box, because the table on which dice would have

The underside of a Dark Green Fritillary showing the subtle green shading and the individual spangles almost like silver.

A Dark Green Fritillary feeding on animal dung.

been played by Romans had a chequered appearance.

This butterfly is single-brooded and flies in midsummer, mainly in grassland. The larvae feed on violets before hibernating until spring.

The poem itself tells the story of why it was written, and is dedicated to my late mother. The 'common' in the poem is Edge Common, otherwise known as Rudge Hill, near Painswick in Gloucestershire, only two valleys away from Slad, of Laurie Lee's *Cider with Rosie* fame. When I walked there with my mother all those years ago there certainly were plenty of Dark Green Fritillaries, and I hope some are still there.

Dark Green Fritillary taking in minerals through its extended proboscis.

Dark Green Fritillary

We walked with our mother one warm August day
uphill to the Common, the fragrant back way
where brambles and bindweed grow strong, full and tall
and midsummer ivy envelopes the wall.

We smelt the fresh hay and heard high skylarks sing
and Mum was the first one to spot, on the wing,
a fast-moving butterfly settle and feed
on luscious and nectar-rich purple-topped weed.

A Dark Green Fritillary – that's what she'd found,
one day years ago on a grassy green mound;
I took her a photo, crouched down on my knee,
and then we went home for digestives and tea.

The picture she hung on the wall by her bed
and glanced up and looked, as she lay there and read,
at the long-past Fritillary live, in its prime,
untouched by the slow stealthy passage of time.

All butterflies really were spirits of men
and women, the Greeks believed, living again,
once gone from this life on their way to find peace
in after-life calm, and serene without cease.

And maybe the last night Mama went to sleep,
in long quiet slumber, the deepest of deep,
she saw the Fritillary, slipped from life's bond,
and walked in the flower-scented meadows beyond.

Dingy Skipper

Erynnis tages

Erynnis is probably a corruption of '*Erinyes*', also known as the Furies, who were terrifying female deities of vengeance in Greek mythology. Being pursued by them was no joke, and could well have prompted the restless and rapid flight characteristic of the butterfly. The *Tages* were Etruscan deities who read the future from the entrails of animals.

It seems cruel to inflict such fearsome names on this small and inoffensive butterfly, which bears an English name that scarcely suggests retribution or animal evisceration.

The Dingy Skipper is a very inconspicuous little creature, and hardly looks like a butterfly at all, being sometimes confused with the wonderfully-named Mother Shipton moth. It is quite small, and a dull brown and grey colour, so it is not surprising that butterfly spotters do not regard it as a glamorous beauty queen.

The larvae of its one generation feed mainly on bird's-foot trefoil and the adults usually fly in May and June on wild open habitats. The sexes are quite similar.

The poem itself comments on the English name.

A freshly-emerged Dingy Skipper
looking curiously moth-like.

The Dingy Skipper with wings closed upright, showing its underside. When roosting in dull weather it can also fold its wings in a very distinctive, curved manner not seen in other butterflies.

Dingy Skipper

You'd think the little Dingy
would live a whinge-tinged life
condemned to cringe
in woodland dinge
and barely reach the forest fringe
while suffering a guilty twinge
for a meadow-flower nectar binge.
But, could nature be so stingy?

It may be a Plain Jane
but in the main
it doesn't thereby suffer pain
because it slips into its other name:
a kipper-coloured dapper
nippy skipper –
Dingy but Skippy.

Duke of Burgundy
Hamearis lucina

This is a rare butterfly, and in this country endangered. It also has unusual names, in both scientific Latin and English. *Lucina* was the Roman goddess of light, the spring and of childbirth. This butterfly does indeed fly in the spring, so that name fits. *Hamearis* is a combination of two Ancient Greek words, together meaning 'at the same time as the spring', and the spring is indeed when this butterfly flies.

The larvae feed on cowslips or primroses, and the adults fly in May and June, then spend the winter as chrysalises before emerging again in the spring.

The English name, which encourages some lepidopterists to refer to it as 'his grace', is of unknown origin. With little supporting evidence I have imagined the butterflies inhabiting a

The Duke of Burgundy looks like a small fritillary, but is no such thing. It is the only representative in Europe of the Riodinidae family – known as the 'metalmarks' due to their silver underwing markings.

medieval Burgundian meadow. This was a remarkable place. For some centuries several states flourished in an area roughly equivalent now with north-eastern France and the Netherlands. In the fifteenth century the Dukes of Burgundy presided over a glittering court and generous patronage of the arts that saw a rich flowering of creativity. The poem tells a little of the story. Norman Davies's book *Vanished Kingdoms* can tell you more.

Duke of Burgundy underside.

Duke of Burgundy

The Dukes of Burgundy, patrons of the arts
were powerful, discriminating,
and ruled over beauty and mustard
from Bruges and Dijon,
their gourmet palates barely satisfied
by feasts of Binchois, Dufay,
the portraits of Van Eyck,
jewelleries and tapestries and cloths of gold.

From these rich nurseries came Josquin,
Josquin des Prés, he of the meadows.
The Dukes banqueted and revelled:
addicts of extravagance
consumers of elegance,
senses illuminated by creative excess.

And in the Duchy's gorgeous emerald fields
the Dukes could ease their aesthetic digestion
and walk beyond the castle walls
through living tapestries of cowslips
where butterfly Dukes still flew in plenty
to feed on simple wild flowers.

A Duke and Duchess making babies in the sunshine.

Essex Skipper

Thymelicus lineola

I was born in Essex, just because my mother happened to be there at the time. I have no other connection with it, and the connection of the Essex Skipper is equally tenuous. It gained its name because it happened to be there when it was first identified here in 1889, although it was soon realised, almost by chance that it could be found in many other areas of southern England.

It is unsurprising that it was not until the nineteenth century that it was recognised as a species distinct from the very similar Small Skipper. The only visible difference between the adult butterflies is the underside of the antennae tips, orange or brown in the Small and black in the Essex. Yealand's stunning photograph illustrates this perfectly. The minute difference might seem trivial, but to a keen lepidopterist it is everything! There is no detail too small for a devotee. Reliable identification can involve a lot of unpoetic crawling about in undergrowth, and an even greater than usual risk of being considered completely crackers by passers-by. I am not even certain that I have ever seen an Essex Skipper.

The adult male differs from the female in having a small sex brand on its forewings. A sex brand is an organ, usually with the appearance of a streak or line on the forewing of a male butterfly, that produces scented pheromones to attract a mate. Their single generation flies in late July and August and the eggs overwinter, with caterpillars feeding on various grasses.

Thymelicus refers to the *thumelikoi*, who were chorus members, dancers, singers, and later on simply entertainers in the ancient world. In the early Greek Christian world, female *thumelikoi* were regarded rather as nightclub lap dancers might be today. They were exciting and 'theatrical', as is the dramatic and energetic flight of this lively estuarine Essex girl, even if our little butterfly is not quite as alluring. *Lineola* is a small line, of which the Essex Skipper has several on its wings.

The Essex Skipper can be mistaken for the similarly-coloured Small Skipper with which it often flies. The black tips to its antennae distinguish it from the Small Skipper.

Essex Skipper

They make all the difference,
those little things;
it's not enough to frisk and dart
and spread cheer among ramblers,
to delight grandchildren
(even though they chase and never catch)
and soothe their elders.

It doesn't suffice to sport
those special up-hinged Skipper wings,
unlike other, common, butterflies,
or to feast on cock's-foot grass.
These are not enough
to be an Essex true-born gal.

You need antennae with black tips
seen only from the front.
So, Small and Large, and Chequered,
Silver-Spotted, Dingy, Grizzled –
all should know their place;
the Essex is different.

Gatekeeper

Pyronia tithonus

This butterfly is also known as Hedge Brown, but the name Gatekeeper is much more interesting, and it can often be seen along gateways, field margins and roadsides in rural England and Wales during July and August. It has one generation and the larvae feed on various grasses before they hibernate. In spring they eat mainly at night until they pupate. The male adult has sex brands on its forewings.

In its youth it is golden-brown, perhaps akin to the glowing embers of a fire. This may have given rise to its scientific name: *Pyronia* is one of the titles given to the Greek goddess Artemis in her role as goddess of fire, in addition to her other guises as goddess of hunting, wild animals and the wilderness, all of which you would suppose would keep her busy enough. She was also a virgin, a state difficult to maintain on Mount Olympus when in the company of so many gods not known for their chaste self-restraint. Being fiery might have helped.

Tithonus was a Trojan prince, who became the lover of the dawn goddess Eos, known to Romans as Aurora. Being immortal she wanted to keep

A female Gatekeeper rests on a blade of grass. Fescues, bents and meadow grasses are its favoured larval food plants.

A male Gatekeeper basking. The brown patches in the middle of his forewings are the sex brands that distinguish him from the female.

Tithonus forever, and persuaded Zeus to make him immortal. Unfortunately she forgot to ask Zeus to stop him ageing, so over the centuries the hapless Tithonus aged and shrivelled dreadfully. He would not have been able to maintain a fulfilling love life with his beloved Eos without a huge supply of Viagra tablets, which had not been invented in ancient times. The poet Tennyson wrote a poem about him.

There is at least some affinity between these Greek names and my poem about a Gatekeeper unlocking lost dreams. The reveries are vivid, recollected in the colours of a dying fire, and they persist long after the events that gave rise to them, enduring but gradually fading with time. Such reflections arose when I was selling a home in Cornwall that I had owned since my children were young. On cliff walks near the cottage we sometimes saw Gatekeeper butterflies, and whenever I see one now it reminds me of those happy days.

Gatekeeper

This is the gatekeeper to the garden of lost dreams,
which do not end when they cannot be real
but when they can no more be dreamed;
then, with luck, a tear may come.

The watercolour on the bedroom wall
of children on the early morning beach
spreads wide into a summer day
not yet lived, maybe never to be lived.

The low drawer in the bow-front chest
glides open of its own accord
and winter gear blows out:
scarves and gloves for windy cliffs,
woollen jumpers, hats and muffs
for bracing walks that may not come.

The climbing rose that could have reached
the guttering, but may do
only when the summer never ends.

The Rayburn now gone cold
in reverie glows hot
as the family thaws along an unknown bench
with mugs of hot brown tea.

And now the walls gaze out on silence.

The terrace by the herb bed,
overgrown with gentle wilderness,
is now transformed in fancy
on a still warm evening in July:
rosé wine and laughter, bats.

When the people long have gone
the dreams live on
as long as they can be divined,
or maybe wakened by the sight
of Gatekeepers roosting
on valerian stems,
and still holding the keys to memory's gates.

Eleanor Glanville
(1654-1709)

It was very unusual in the Restoration period in Britain for a woman to become a well-known scientist, but Eleanor Glanville achieved it. She was born at Tickenham Court in Somerset, a few miles south of Bristol, and not far from the home of the author of this book. She lived in turbulent times: in 1654, the year of her birth, Oliver Cromwell was still ruling the country, and Eleanor's father had been an officer in the Roundhead army, but Charles II returned to claim his throne just a few years later. Eleanor inherited some wealth from her father, and as a gentlewoman was given the unofficial courtesy title 'Lady', even though she was not formally entitled to it. She then married an artist from Lincolnshire and moved there with him. It was in that part of the world that she became interested in insects, and especially butterflies.

While roaming the Wolds in her new home she found the butterfly that she called Lincolnshire Fritillary, but which was later named after her, Glanville Fritillary. There is only one other native British butterfly named after a lepidopterist, and that is the summer form of the Comma butterfly, which is paler than the earlier brood. Its scientific Latin name is *Polygonia* c-album *hutchinsoni*, named after another female lepidopterist, Emma Hutchinson, who lived in Herefordshire in the 19th century, and was the wife of a vicar. She could deserve a section all to herself, but there is not room in this book.

After her first husband died, Eleanor was married again to a Mr Glanville. He was violent and abusive towards her, so it is ironic that it is his name that is now immortalised in the Glanville Fritillary butterfly, although I prefer to think that it is her name, even if borrowed from him. He was mainly interested in her wealth, but she would have none of it and spent her time studying butterflies.

She became well-known in scientific circles in London and was friendly with some of the leading butterfly enthusiasts of her day. After she died she suffered the indignity of having her will successfully challenged under the Acts of Lunacy of her day, on the grounds that only an insane woman could possibly have been interested in collecting butterflies. This posthumous indignity has not prevented her from being remembered as a remarkable and learned woman. She is the subject of a novel by Fiona Mountain, published in 2009, *The Lady of the Butterflies*.

The Eleanor Glanville Centre is an interdisciplinary centre for inclusion, diversity and equality at the University of Lincoln. What a shame that no such institution existed in the 18th century!

Glanville Fritillary
Melitaea cinxia

This butterfly is named in English after Lady Eleanor Glanville, who was born in a village just a few miles from where I live. Some of her story is told in my poem and there is more detail in the mini-biography (*opposite*).

   Several possible derivations for the first part of the scientific name of the Glanville Fritillary have been suggested. The least unlikely meaning for *Melitaea* is 'honeyed', perhaps alluding to the love of sweet nectar that this butterfly has, as indeed do most butterflies. *Cinxia* was one of the names given to the Roman goddess Juno in her role as goddess of childbirth. The cingulum was

Glanville Fritillary roosting, showing its beautiful cream and orange bands with black markings on the underwings.

a belt worn by a bride to symbolise the bond with her husband. It was tied with a knot of Hercules, which was very difficult to untie. The goddess Cinxia was able to unloose such bride-girdles, and the untying of the knot represented the loss of the bride's virginity.

Glanville Fritillaries now occur in Britain only on and near the Isle of Wight, and until recently at Sand Point in Somerset. They were much more widely distributed when Eleanor Glanville found them while escaping from her abusive husband. The butterflies need very particular conditions, where there is plenty of plantain food plant in a coastland habitat at the right temperature at the right times. Glanvilles are fussy, and that is one reason why they are so locally restricted. They have one brood, with adults flying in May and June. The larvae hibernate in communal groups and pupate in the spring. The sexes are similar.

It is one of the prettiest of the Fritillaries, as you will see from the photograph, with bright and intricate silver and golden brown patterns under their wings. We know very little about the looks of the woman after whom it is named. The photo on page 50 is of Tiffany Haynes dressed as Eleanor Glanville might have looked in the seventeenth century.

Glanville Fritillary

The Lady Eleanor Glanville,
woman of standing and wealth,
excised her son from her last will
feeling he damaged her health.

Her husband wanted to shoot her,
never with any success;
she suffered much for her gender,
prisoner of cruel duress.

Because her life was so bruising,
butterflies helped her keep calm:
she toured the counties observing,
keeping herself out of harm.

And so she found a fritillary
no one had previously named -
but then was scolded and pilloried
even though now she is famed.

Her will was shamefully challenged:
butterfly minds thought unhinged;
Eleanor Glanville, though strange,
still after death took revenge.

Her name lives on as reminder –
Glanville the lady is gone,
but insect presences of her
out in the meadows fly on.

Glanville Fritillary, upperside.
Its favoured larval food plant on the
coastal slopes of the Isle of Wight
is ribwort plantain.

Grayling
Hipparchia semele

The Grayling tends to live on coastal cliffs, stony heathland and even derelict industrial sites. There is just one brood, with larvae feeding on grasses and then hibernating. The adult flies in July and August, and is often unseen until it takes to the wing when approached.

Hipparchus was an ancient Greek astronomer who mapped the stars and planets and calculated ways to predict their movements. In this butterfly name he is incongruously linked with Semele, who in Greek mythology was one of Zeus's many girlfriends, and the only mortal ever to bear him a child, in this case his son, Dionysos. Known by the Romans as Bacchus, Dionysos was god of the grape harvest, winemaking and ritual madness.

Semele was a Theban princess and priestess. She was sacrificing a bull one day (she must have been seriously strong) when Zeus saw her and fell in love. This was a frequent occurrence with him, and usually did not last long. Semele became pregnant, and made the mistake of confiding in the wife of Zeus, Hera, who was no less jealous in this instance of her husband's infidelity than usual. Hera hinted to Semele that Zeus's infatuation would not last, and so Semele asked him to prove his affection by appearing in his full glory. Sadly, she forgot that mortals could not survive the blinding light of the king of the gods. She was burnt to a cinder, and Hera had her vengeance, at least until Zeus took his next paramour. The story was not quite over, because Semele's son Dionysos rescued her from Hades, the Greek underworld, and she became a goddess on Mount Olympus.

There is little hint of Bacchanalian frenzy or flashing thunderbolts in the flight of the Grayling butterfly. The English name gives a more accurate description, although the colour grey does not do justice to the delicate silver and stone camouflage of its underwings. Both Graylings in the photographs have their wings closed. This is their habitual posture when at rest.

A Grayling in typical resting position on bare earth with its wings closed. No eyespot is visible.

Grayling

Grey, with sticks,
two walkers edge along the brink of earth
where cliffs crumble into foam,
and they hope that summer may survive.

They chance on faded, wing-torn
Graylings almost underfoot,
that rise from dry-baked earth
to dance a leisurely duet.

The Graylings know no age, no past
no history, no future
neither the walkers', nor their own
as if no end will come.

Four heavy boots imprint their record
in the silvery cliff-top dust
left by watermarked desiccated wings
of countless Grayling generations.

Grayling underside, this time with the eyespot visible to frighten away predators.

The Green Hairstreak resting on plantain in its usual posture with wings closed.

Green Hairstreak
Callophrys rubi

This little butterfly is another of the Hairstreak family and its cousins also appear in this book. Hairstreaks are so called because they tend to have transverse streaks on the under-surface of the wings and delicate, hair-like tails on their hindwings. The poem itself refers to the appearance of the Green Hairstreak, named for the green underside of its wings.

Depending on habitat, its food plants can include rock rose, gorse, bramble and bilberry. There is one generation, with adults flying in May and June, and it overwinters as a chrysalis. The sexes look similar but behave differently, with males darting out to find mates while females stay near food plants when laying eggs.

The scientific name, roughly translated, means 'beautiful eyebrows of the bramble plant'. *Kallos* is Greek for 'beauty', and *ophrus* 'eyebrow'. This composite name may refer to the tiny

A new, bright Green Hairstreak specimen displaying its emerald green underwings.

filament-hairs that cover part of the body. *Rubus*, which comes from the Latin for 'red', is a genus of plants that includes the blackberry, one of the food plants.

Green Hairstreaks are notoriously difficult to spot, even though they occur quite widely, because their colours blend so perfectly with their surroundings. They always settle with wings closed, so only the green underside is visible. The brown upperside can only be seen when they are flying, and even then only a glimpse. The poem refers to this shyness about their more colourful side. They seem to lose their green scales quickly, so finding a photogenic specimen is not always easy. Yealand has succeeded with his lovely picture (*opposite*).

The colour of the wings is produced by light refraction in their wing scales, and they sparkle in sunshine.

Green Hairstreak

A streak of emerald flashes on the broom;
a Hairstreak searches for a dulcet bloom
and blends with leaves as settled wings are green
– its upper brown is hardly ever seen.

Ambiguous, it could be beast or weed
or some unheard-of kind of hybrid breed,
its secret motivations well concealed
in bush and shrub and brambles of the field.

It hints, suggests, a flicker on the gorse,
a fleeting presence on its cryptic course,
and this is how it will confound belief
– this creature's more than just a flying leaf.

Green Hairstreak, underside. A slim strip of the brown upperside is just visible to the right.

Green-veined White

Pieris napi

I hope, reader, that you will not think me heartless for writing my poem about the Green-veined White in flippant mode. It always makes me a little sad to find dying or dead butterflies, perhaps because I am reminded of my own mortality, but I try to remind myself that their lives are short, and that finding one dead does at least mean that it was once alive. Like almost any insect, a butterfly is vulnerable to predation by birds, animals, humans, disease and, in this case, a spider. When I wrote the verses, I was thinking of the kind of old-fashioned holiday cottage of my youth, which sometimes had an outside loo festooned with spiders' webs and littered with the half-eaten bodies of their prey. They were a far cry from modern holiday lets with superfast broadband and ninety-inch televisions.

This butterfly is a cousin of the Large and Small butterflies that also appear elsewhere in this book. Superficially it can appear quite similar to the Small White, but its underwings bear mottled greenish-grey vein markings that help to differentiate it. The effect is produced by a mixture of black and yellow spots. The light shining through its wings in the photograph on page 62 illustrates this perfectly.

Pieris was Ancient Greek for a Muse, of whom according to legend there were nine. They were daughters of Zeus, living near Mount Olympus in Greece, and were the semi-divine inspirers of creative artists of various kinds. Several of the Muses were specifically connected with the inspiration of poetry. My own Muse would probably have been Thalia, because she was the Muse of pastoral poetry, as well as comedy. Butterflies do fly in the countryside and they do make me smile with pleasure. There is more about Thalia in the commentary on the Heath Fritillary.

The *napi* part of its name comes from *Brassica napus*, the oilseed rape plant, which is one of the food plants of the Green-veined White larvae, and which, in its cultivated form, fills many summer fields with bright yellow colour.

The caterpillars of this butterfly are much less likely than those of their cousins, the Large White and Small White (otherwise known as 'Cabbage Whites'), to munch their way through the carefully nurtured greens in your kitchen garden. This is because Green-veined Whites prefer wild members of the *Crucifera* family, such as garlic mustard or cuckooflower.

**Green-veined White nectaring
on cuckoo flower.**

Green-veined White

The Green-veined White was a sorry sight
in the outside loo at the side;
with one wing caught it was quite distraught,
and before too long it had died.

This Green-veined White was a morbid sight
in the graveyard over the loo;
the spider's web was a fearsome trap
and its strands as sticky as glue.

Among the corpses of wasps and flies,
the torn-off heads and the legs,
where all that flies is doomed, and dies,
there was nothing left but the dregs.

Above the bowl,
* on the privy chain,*
was a large fat spider
* asleep,*
and down below,
* by the blocked-up drain,*
were the corpses inches deep.

The Green-veined White was
* a long time dead,*
but the spider fulsomely fed.

The underside of a Green-veined White clearly showing the grey streaks that give it a greenish impression. It has green eyes with black dots.

Grizzled Skipper
Pyrgus malvae

This little butterfly is a cousin of the Dingy Skipper, bearing an English name that is not much more complimentary than the Dingy's. It likes various habitats, including downland and open woodland. There is one brood, with adults flying in May and June. They overwinter as pupae to emerge in the late spring.

Pyrgos is the name of several places in Greece, although we do not know whether this was in the mind of the scientist who gave the name. One of them is on the island of Santorini, in ancient times known as Thera. Nowadays it is a spectacularly beautiful holiday destination, but thousands of years ago a gigantic volcanic eruption devastated the island. It is thought that the resulting outpouring of volcanic ash and tsunami contributed to the decline of the ancient Minoan civilisation on the island of Crete a little further south. There may even have been Grizzled Skippers on the island when it exploded. Pyrgos also means tower or rampart in ancient Greek, but this does not help us very much.

Underside of a Grizzled Skipper as it roosts in early morning on a wet flowerhead.

A Grizzled Skipper
settles on a dandelion.
This small butterfly,
with its distinctive
chequer-board
patterning, is not much
bigger than a human
thumb joint.

Malvae means 'of the mallow-plant', a plant on which the larvae of this butterfly definitely do *not* feed. They prefer agrimony or wild strawberry. So, a tenuous classical allusion associated with the wrong flower, and therefore perfect for the imagination.

Grizzled Skipper

The Grizzled Skipper's life is short
– it's lucky if it's thirty days;
a Skipper's day in human time
would feel like several years.

This lively beast is Grizzled from the start,
already conscious of its age,
though not with silver locks
or grey-tinged beard
but enamelled chequered wings.

It moves too quickly to be seen
except from corner of the eye
an almost-imagined glint
in the late Spring sun,
dancing to the last stretched
Skipper-day
as it looks for a safe place to die.

Heath Fritillary

Melitaea athalia

Even that fount of classical erudition, Maitland Emmet, is unsure about the derivation of *Melitaea*, (see also page 51) but it seems possible that it is connected with honey or mead, the drink made from honey. As Heath Fritillaries, like all butterflies, like to feed on honey-sweet nectar, this is a reasonable guess. There are two goddesses named *Thalia* to choose from in Greek mythology (see also page 60). One was amongst the nine Muses, already mentioned in connection with the Glanville Fritillary, and was the goddess of comedy and idyllic poetry. She is often portrayed crowned with ivy and wearing elegant boots, and sometimes holds a bugle or trumpet. The other was one of three Graces, and presided over youth, beauty and happiness.

Whichever of these deities was included in this butterfly name, she was young, pretty and full of fun, and likely to brighten the day of any lepidopterist almost as much as the sight of a rare Heath Fritillary. The modern butterfly is one of this country's severely endangered species, only occurring in a very small number of locations, and surviving mainly because of the active intervention of conservationists.

I have already explained the origin of the name 'Fritillary'. The butterflies do indeed fly on heaths, as well as coppiced woodland. It was at one such heath, on Exmoor, that I found my first Heath Fritillary when walking with my family some years ago. Unfortunately, after wading through bracken to chase after butterflies we all became infested with ticks and had to visit the local hospital to have them removed, but it was such a joy to be able to see one of our rarest butterflies.

Yealand's photograph is taken from an unusual angle – the underneath. The butterfly is clinging precariously to a grass stalk, with its wings wide open. Its flight period is from May until August, depending on where it is in the country. The larvae feed mainly on cow-wheat, and hibernate in leaf litter to pupate in the spring. They have only one brood.

My poem is short and to the point. The haiku originated as a Japanese verse form. In a common version of it there are strict rules about the number of syllables in each line. Strictly speaking the haiku should not make use of metaphorical imagery, but I have broken this rule just for once in my short piece, because I felt that the poem called out for it.

A Heath Fritillary displays its underwings as it rests on a grass stem in late afternoon.

Heath Fritillary

Haiku

*Rare amber Heath wings
gather sun to chase away
sudden summer gloom.*

The Heath Fritillary, one of Britain's rarest butterflies, was on the brink of extinction in the 1970s. It has held on in a few colonies in the West Country and in Essex and Kent where more enlightened habitat management has enabled its survival.

High Brown Fritillary
Argynnis adippe

The High Brown Fritillary is a close relative of the Dark Green Fritillary which is also featured in this book. On the wing they are very difficult to tell apart, but when they settle, their underwings are different. Where the Dark Green has a patch of dark green under its wings, the High Brown has a row of brown spots between the outer margin and the silver spangles, and this may have given rise to the 'High Brown' part of the name. These spots are clearly visible in Yealand's photograph (see page 70).

The larvae, like those of many other Fritillaries, feed on violets, having hatched from overwintered eggs in the spring. They reach adulthood in midsummer, flying between June and August.

Argynnis is one of the many names for Aphrodite, the ancient Greek goddess of love and beauty. It is suggested that this name may originally have come from Indian lore, and refers to the brilliance of the dawn. She was the goddess of love, beauty and passion, and in one version of her story was born out of sea-foam, as depicted in Botticelli's *Birth of Venus*. Venus was the name given to her by the Romans.

She had an adventurous existence ('life' not being the right word for an immortal deity). For a start she was involved in the outbreak of the Trojan war, and was also so attractive that libidinous gods fought over her, prompting Zeus to marry her off to Hephaestus, in an attempt to

High Brown Fritillary feeding on knapweed.

stop the squabbling. As her husband, the god of blacksmiths and fire, was so ugly, she was frequently tempted into extra-marital affairs with better-looking men. These liaisons led to the births of Hermaphroditos, who was an early exemplar of gender ambiguity, and Priapos, who lived in a state of permanent arousal that would have been the envy of any sufferer from erectile dysfunction.

Adippe appears to be an invented name with no obvious meaning.

My poem follows the strict form of the pantoum, and refers to one of the reasons why the High Brown Fritillary has become so rare. I count myself lucky to have seen specimens in the wild, some years ago, on the Malvern Hills, and I dearly hope they can survive there. Its remaining strongholds are in western England, including Morecambe Bay in the north, through parts of the Welsh borders to Exmoor and Dartmoor in the south. It is a very beautiful butterfly that is still in severe danger of extinction in this country.

A High Brown Fritillary showing the distinctive ginger-brown rings enclosing the small 'pearls'. These are not present on its cousin the Dark Green Fritillary.

High Brown Fritillary

Pantoum

I am not green or low, but brown and high,
no common insect, easy to be found;
I am a rather special butterfly,
though badly threatened, still just holding ground.

No common insect, easy to be found,
much rarer now than my close Dark Green kin;
though badly threatened, still just holding ground,
we share our evolutionary origin.

Much rarer now than my close Dark Green kin,
I used to roam and breed throughout the land;
we share our evolutionary origin,
but why I've suffered I don't understand.

I used to roam and breed throughout the land,
until the shadows fell across my world,
but why I've suffered I don't understand,
especially as my wings are orange-pearled.

Until the shadows fell across my world
I felt an ornament of nature's art,
especially as my wings are orange-pearled,
but now I have become a being apart.

I felt an ornament of nature's art,
but then the bracken grew too wide and tall,
so I have become a being apart
and barely cling to life at all.

So then the bracken grew too wide and tall;
my violets struggle in the deathly shade
and barely cling to life at all,
while in the meadows flowers wilt and fade.

My violets struggle in the deathly shade –
outmoded coppice-cutting was not done,
while in the meadows flowers wilt and fade,
deprived of precious nectar-giving sun.

Outmoded coppice-cutting was not done;
I was not favoured by the human gods,
deprived of precious nectar-giving sun,
yet even so survive against the odds.

I was not favoured by the human gods,
unlike my cousins, left to fail and die,
yet even so survive against the odds;
I am not green or low, but brown and high.

Holly Blue
Celastrina argiolus

The scientific Latin name for this butterfly is *Celastrina*, derived from the Greek for 'holly', which is part of the English name for the butterfly. *Argiolus* is a diminutive of 'Argus', whom we have met already.

It is called 'Holly Blue' because the larvae of its spring generation feed on holly. The summer generation prefer ivy, and its larvae then overwinter as pupae. It varies cyclically in abundance from year to year because of attack by a small parasitic wasp, but it still appears in my Somerset garden every spring. The adults can be seen in most parts of Britain, although rarely in Scotland. The females have a darker band at the edges of their wings than the males.

Because of their affinity with evergreens I sometimes think of the butterflies when I am decorating the house with holly or ivy leaves at Christmas time. This is how they became linked in my mind with the well-known Christmas carol, and gave rise to the poem. For many centuries holly and ivy have been used as Christmas decorations, in part because they retain their green colour when many plants have lost their leaves. They are a symbol of continuing life during the coldest and darkest part of the year.

The Christian churches have often extended this symbolism to give it religious meaning, and in the traditional carol the holly is supposed to represent Jesus Christ and the ivy the Virgin Mary, his mother. My poem intends no disrespect to the Christian beliefs reflected in the carol, and is simply a joyful celebration of a beautiful creature that cheers us during the youthful months of the year.

The butterfly in Yealand's photograph has the lovely pale eggshell blue of its species and is having a good feed, with its proboscis curling firmly into the flower where it is perched.

A Holly Blue feeds on bramble. Unlike many other blues it has no red or orange spots.

A Holly Blue at rest on holly. The black edges of the forewings show that this is a female.

Holly Blue

The Holly Blue loves ivy
and loves the holly too;
the holly's green, the ivy's green,
so why's the Holly Blue?

The holly bears a bloom
as white as lily flower
and there she lays her springtime eggs
within their budding bower.

The holly bears a berry
as red as any blood,
but Holly Blue is palest blue
and holly is its infant food.

The holly bears a prickle
as sharp as any thorn,
and yet in this unlikely place
the young of Blues are born.

The holly bears a bark
as bitter as any gall,
but this is where their young grow up
and where their caterpillars crawl.

The holly and the ivy
now both are full well grown;
the swallows left and fields are mown
and Holly Blues have fed and flown.

But evergreens are evergreen,
the Holly Blue is ever blue;
where field meets sky
is where the green meets blue.

Large Blue

Maculinea arion

A female Large Blue rests on clover at Daneway Banks in Gloucestershire.

The Large Blue is not large compared with many butterflies, but is the largest among the British Blues, and possibly the most famous. It has a remarkable history in Britain, having been driven to extinction in the 1970s by habitat loss associated with changes in animal grazing practices that had occurred over a long period.

One of Britain's most distinguished lepidopterists, Professor Jeremy Thomas, spent many years researching the Large Blue butterfly, and discovered that it has an extraordinary life cycle. The larvae of Large Blues first of all feed on wild thyme, and then are tended by a particular species of small red ants, which carry the larvae into their nests, where they hibernate. Once there, the Large Blue larvae repay the generous hospitality of their red ant hosts by eating their larvae. In effect they are parasites. Eventually, having fooled the long-suffering red ants, the Large Blues pupate then emerge from underground nests and fly in June and July. There is just one brood. If the reader is interested in the scientific detail, there is an article by Professor Thomas listed in the bibliography of this book.

With the information provided by this (literally) ground-breaking research, conservationists led by Thomas were able to create managed nature reserves where the right conditions existed for Large Blues and their red ant servants to thrive. Butterflies were reintroduced from Sweden and, within a few years, Large Blues were flying again in a number of sites in southern England, including some where they had previously occurred. Coastal sites at or near Millook, Morwenstow, Boscastle and Bude were some of the locations in Cornwall where they used to fly.

Arion was a mythological ancient Greek poet who is supposed to have invented the *Dithyram*, a hymn sung and danced in honour of the god of wine and fertility. He came from either Lesbos or Corinth. Most agree, however, that he was kidnapped by pirates and later miraculously rescued by dolphins, as one is, of course. The word *Maculinea* is a combination of *maculo*, meaning to speckle or mottle, and *linea*, a line, referring to the line of dark dots on the wings of the Large Blue. Recently the scientific name has changed to *Phengaris arion*.

I wrote the poem before the wonderful return of this very pretty butterfly. It is not quite scientifically accurate, because although over-collecting was not helpful, it was not the primary cause of the now temporary extinction of the Large Blue. When, eventually, I saw live Large Blues in Somerset it was an emotional moment. There will be another poem about that day sometime.

Below: the female Large Blue is usually a fraction larger than the male and with slightly more prominent markings.

Opposite page: Large Blues mating.

Large Blue

The clergyman
the lawyer's son,
nannies, grannies
with flowered hats
and ribboned plaits,
mad professors
priest confessors
the curious,
injurious
all came to look
around Millook
or Morwenstow

where west winds blow
for Maculinea Arion
to satisfy their predilection
for butterfly collection.

The Large Blues were pursued
from Boscastle to Bude,
their bodies pinned
their numbers thinned.

They could not hide
and so they died
murdered in the end
by caring loving friends
with greedy care
to keep them rare.

But still they fly
in my mind's eye,
on dark wings roam
across their ancient home
my mind to haunt
their killers taunt
with freedom yet
from captors' net.

Large Heath
Coenonympha tullia

In Britain the Large Heath occurs in Wales, Scotland and northern England on boggy heaths, where its larvae feed mainly on hare's-tail cottongrass. They hibernate as larvae and then pupate, with the adults flying between June and August in one generation.

The Large Heath butterfly is related to the Small Heath, with which it shares the first part of its scientific name, *Coenonympha*. This is from Greek and, translated literally, means 'common' (as in 'shared') nymph or nature spirit. I doubt that the name was intended to hint at promiscuous practices among ancient nymphs; it may perhaps suggest commonality with other similar species. *Tullia* was a Roman name, and research finds that there are plenty from whom to choose, including the last queen of Rome, the daughter of a Roman statesman, an Italian sixteenth century poet, and many others. Unfortunately none of them appears to bear any relation to Large Heath butterflies, so this is probably another rather random invention.

My poem is written in a variant of the sestina form, which dates from twelfth century troubadours and more recently has been used by poets as diverse as Rudyard Kipling and Ezra Pound. It celebrates the lives of a few of the illustrious humans of the butterfly world. Linnaeus was mentioned in the preface to this book, and is credited with creating the naming system that is still used today.

Sir Winston Churchill, Britain's wartime leader, was said to be a keen butterfly enthusiast and tried, unsuccessfully, to re-introduce the Black-veined White butterfly, which had previously become extinct in this country, to his country estate at Chartwell. He, along with Miriam Rothschild and Vladimir Nabokov, have their own mini-biographies in this book.

Lewis Carroll, of *Alice's Adventures in Wonderland* fame, needs no introduction, and, in *Through the Looking-Glass and What Alice Found There*, Alice encounters some insects:

'*Crawling at your feet,*' said the Gnat (Alice drew her feet back in some alarm), '*you may observe a Bread-and-Butterfly. Its wings are thin slices of Bread-and-butter, its body is a crust, and its head is a lump of sugar.*'

Large Heath, underside. This specimen, with large brown spots, is from the subspecies *davus* and found in north-west and central England.

Large Heath
Sestina

In Greece the psyche was a soul on wings
and since that time a multitude has flown,
each butterfly a spirit of the dead,
each soul refashioned into different life
from villains, heroes, humans bad and good;
but can a Large Heath know whose soul it bears?

There is a name that every butterfly bears
for life, from egg until full-grown on wings.
Linnaeus aimed to name all that had flown,
and some that through extinction now are dead;
perhaps he chose a Large Heath for new life
to live in lepidoptery for good.

Sir Winston thought that butterflies were good
for soothing stresses that a human bears:
his troubles could be borne away on wings
while in the sky the fighter planes had flown,
to show Churchillian spirit was not dead,
protecting British shores and way of life.

Miriam Rothschild gave much of her life
to the natural world, for the greater good;
she braved the Transylvanian mountain bears
to search for her beloved jewels on wings,
for her amongst the loveliest that have flown,
and even precious in a jar stone dead.

The dreamer Lewis Carroll, now long dead,
is still remembered as he brought to life
his dreamland characters in tales so good
they entered folklore; and still now he bears
the honour of inventing food on wings,
though 'bread-and-butterfly' has never flown.

Nabokov's lifelong love was not high-flown –
he treasured butterflies alive or dead,
as scientist, writer, artist gave them life,
his practicality all to the good;
he felt the burdens that an exile bears,
but still his soul flew high on creative wings.

Good lepidopterists, they are not dead;
their souls have flown and found new life on wings,
and memory bears witness to their deeds.

Large Heath resting on a bracken frond.

King Boris III of Bulgaria
(1894-1943)

Boris Clement Robert Mary Pius Louis Stanislaus Xavier was King of Bulgaria between the wars and during the first part of the Second World War. He was also a lover of butterflies, flowers and the natural world, as well as railway locomotives. Bulgaria in the eastern Balkans has a warm summer climate and contains some fine mountain landscapes. Many of these in the 1930s were even less affected by urbanisation or intensive farming and less contaminated by insecticide pollution than is the case nowadays, so there must have been plenty of butterflies. Even now the Rila National Park, mentioned in my poem, is a favoured destination for butterfly and wildlife holidays.

Boris's father, King Ferdinand, was also an amateur naturalist, and accumulated an extensive collection of butterflies. He must have passed on this passion to his son, possibly on joint rambles in the mountains. Ferdinand was a personal friend of Walter Rothschild, also featured in this book. Boris was unlucky enough to be king at a turbulent time, when fascism and Nazi Germany were destroying the peace of Europe. For a while he was effectively a royal dictator in his own country, and to escape from the inevitable pressures involved he would walk out looking for butterflies.

After Bulgaria was threatened with either destruction or occupation, in 1941 Boris reluctantly allied his country with Nazi Germany. It was only a matter of time before Hitler was demanding that the Jews of Bulgaria, like those of many other countries under his control or influence, should be sent to the death camps. Boris, like many of his compatriots, was horrified by this, but it was not clear whether it would be possible to prevent it from happening. Many Jews from Bulgarian-occupied Macedonia were sent by the Nazis to their deaths, and King Boris was not able or willing to stop this happening. But when Hitler's attention was turned towards Bulgaria itself Boris used many stratagems to try to stop it. It is estimated that his actions may have saved up to fifty thousand Jewish people from extermination.

King Boris paid a heavy personal price for this. Following a visit to Hitler in 1943, during which he caused the Führer to fly into a rage after defying him, he returned to Bulgaria but died in mysterious circumstances soon afterwards. It was widely believed that he had been poisoned. The book Hitler and the King, by John Hall Spencer, tells the full story.

Bulgaria also paid a heavy price for having been on the losing side in the war. The Soviet Red Army of Stalin's Russia invaded and occupied the country, imposing a Communist regime that lasted for several decades before it collapsed. After the Communists had been overthrown, Boris's son Simeon returned from exile to Bulgaria and briefly became Prime Minister. As I write, Simeon still lives and despite his old age should be able to walk in some of the same butterfly meadows that his father loved so much.

Large Skipper
Ochlodes venata

This is another of the eight Skippers that appear in this book. They are a large family, with dozens more relatives globally. 'Skipper' is an appropriate name because all the Skippers seem to skip and whir through the countryside. They are easy to spot, although it is often difficult to distinguish one from another.

In this country Large Skippers occur widely in the countryside, but also in parks and churchyards, wherever there is the right kind of grass to feed its larvae. The adults fly mainly in June and July, though not in most of Scotland. There is one generation a year, and larvae overwinter in specially formed tubes of grass. The sexes are similar except that males have a black line through the centre of their forewing. It is one of the few British butterflies that appears to have widened its range in recent times.

Ochlodes is Ancient Greek for 'turbulent', and *venatus* is Latin for the art and practice of hunting, so the scientific name suggests a very energetic insect that hunts, no doubt for sweet nectar.

It may seem odd to write a poem about King Boris III of Bulgaria in connection with the Large Skipper, but I explain why in the separate profile of him. I have visited the beautiful Rila monastery in Bulgaria, mentioned in the poem, where the heart

A Large Skipper resting on lady's bedstraw.

A male Large Skipper showing the dark marking in the centre of the forewing which is its sex brand, or androconial organ.

of King Boris is buried. It is surrounded by mountain slopes that, in season, would have been alive with butterflies. Many butterflies to be found there are far more exotic than the Large Skipper that is the subject of the poem, but this is a book about British butterflies.

A little further to the east lie the Rhodope mountains, named after Queen Rhodope of Thrace, who, according to legend, was turned into a mountain along with her husband by Zeus and Hera because they had offended the gods.

Large Skipper

King Boris the third of Bulgaria loved his people
and his nation's butterflies;
in the high Rhodope mountains
the summer flowers brightened
if he strode by with his net
and his spirits soared high in the peaks
as if on the wings of a Skipper, Ochlodes venata.

Ochlodes, the bringer of turbulent times,
all the same distracting Boris's troubled mind
from the horrors of war
and Hitler's evil scheming threats.

Venata, the art of hunting –
Boris stopped the hunting of his country's Jews,
but then himself became the hunted.

Nazi poison took his life but spared him
from the later sight of Stalin's jackboots
stamping the streets of Sofia.

They put his heart at Rila monastery
but his soul stayed on the mountain slopes,
content amid the ceaseless whir of Skipper wings.

Male Large Skipper showing its upperside.

Lulworth Skipper
Thymelicus acteon

Here is another Skipper, but this one is much more rare. It was first identified near the village of Lulworth in Dorset in 1832, and it still flies along coastline nearby, occurring nowhere else in Britain. The British Army has tank firing ranges near Lulworth, and here tiny, fragile Lulworth Skippers co-exist with the heavy weapons of war. This extraordinary juxtaposition inspired me to write the poem. It has one brood and flies from July to September, overwintering as a larva. The adult male is darker than the female, and has a sex brand on each forewing.

A *thumelikos* was a member of the chorus and a dancer in ancient Greek tragedy. Skippers dance when they fly. *Actaeon* was a hunter from Greek mythology. There are several different versions of the tale of how he came to his rather unpleasant end, but the one most commonly cited is that when he was out hunting he came across the virgin goddess of hunting, Artemis, bathing in a woodland pool. He was so struck by her beauty that he could not resist looking at her admiringly. Artemis was understandably

Lulworth Skipper holding forewings and hindwings angled apart – a posture typical of many skippers.

cross with him, as ladies sometimes are when strange men stare at them in woodland pools, and forbade him to speak, so that he could not describe what he had seen. His punishment, if he did speak, was to be transformed into a stag. When he heard his hounds barking for him he called out to them, was turned into a stag and became the prey of his own hounds. They had a jolly good meal and he was snuffed out in a few crunching mouthfuls.

The Lulworth Skippers hunt only for their larval food plant, tor-grass, and other good nectar sources. If, however, they are unlucky enough to be hit by an exploding tank shell they are blown to smithereens, a doleful fate that is at least quicker than being torn apart by hunting dogs.

Opposite: The Lulworth Skipper, the smallest of the 'golden' Skippers of the UK, is confined to the calcareous grasslands along the coast of south Dorset.

Lulworth Skipper

Metallic larvae advance
across abandoned Dorset fields,
creatures spawned from fissures
in paranoid minds of war-planners;
they crush at random, living and the dead,
consuming peace with guttural aggression.

The tanks of Lulworth Camp
turn their turrets in anger,
and with unnatural commotion
hurl fiery bolts at innocent hillsides,
home of yellow-bordered
green larvae of the field.

Afterwards, summer raindrops
cool the now-quiet barrels.
A soldier lifts the hatch and drinks his tea,
while on the muzzle, for a moment,
rests a Lulworth Skipper, before he quickly flees
to find a peaceful clump of Dorset tor-grass.

Marbled White

Melanargia galathea

The English and scientific Latin names of this butterfly are partly descriptive. Its wings are white and have black markings on them that give an impression of marbling. Technically the Marbled White is a member of the Browns family, but only the female has any brown colouring (see the photograph on page 90). Yealand's lovely picture shows a couple mating. This male has black markings and the female a rather fetching café-au-lait pattern. Butterfly colours do vary somewhat, but this butterfly is usually easy to identify.

There is one generation a year and adults fly mainly in June and July in grassy places such as woodland rides and road verges in England and southern Wales. The larvae hibernate as soon as they hatch and in the spring feed on red fescue grass before pupating. In some grassy places it may be possible to see a lot of them, especially if there is also an abundance of the purple flowers that the adults seem to like so much.

In earlier times the English name for the Marbled White was 'Half-Mourner', probably because it was only partly black, but I have always thought of it as a cheerful butterfly, associated in my mind with midsummer rambles. *Melanargia* is the joining of the two Greek words for black and white, which is entirely appropriate. *Galatea* was a divine nereid, or sea-nymph, who loved the mortal Acis. When he was killed by the cyclops Polyphemus, Galatea transformed the blood of Acis into a Sicilian river and he became a river spirit. Not a bad way to go, I suppose.

The Acis and Galatea story has been very popular with various artists and composers, with Lully, Handel and Haydn all writing operas on the subject. My poem does not dwell on ancient murders or water spirits and describes the butterflies roosting and waking.

A Marbled White warming
itself on bracken.

Marbled White

There are voices from the grasslands
of butterflies that cannot speak aloud –
whispers hover on a wafting breeze
and cling to long stalks,
while the summer dusk weeps
its crystal tears on their folded wings.

In the morning sun there is the slightest sigh
of patterned Whites as they marble the air
and dissolve in streaks and spots;
though voiceless, they proclaim
with confidence their birthright
as they striate the greenscape country.

Marbled Whites mating on creeping thistle. The brownish butterfly is the female, the blacker one the male. She is feeding well, and is perhaps bored?

Marsh Fritillary

Eurodryas aurinia

There are other Fritillaries in this book; see Dark Green Fritillary for a commentary on the English name 'Fritillary'. One habitat favoured by Marsh Fritillaries is damp grassland, hence 'Marsh' in its name. Rather perversely, it also likes chalky slopes. It has one brood and typically flies from May to July. Larvae overwinter in that form and pupate in the spring.

Eurodryas joins together 'euro', or European (which had a different meaning in ancient Greece), and 'dryas', a wood-nymph. Nymphs appear a lot in butterfly names, and must have been everywhere in ancient times, peeping through the bushes and frolicking in mountain streams. According to the Roman historian Tacitus, who mentions *Aurinia* in one of his works, she was a Germanic queen priestess. This is a rare appearance of Northern European mythology in butterfly lore, and reflects the considerable rarity of this butterfly.

The main food plant of the Marsh Fritillary is devil's-bit scabious. Old folktales have it that the Devil was angry about the purported capability of scabious to cure scabies, and tried to destroy the plant by biting off the roots, hence 'devil's-bit(ten)'. Satan makes a guest appearance in the poem.

The Marsh Fritillary has been in severe decline and is now restricted to only a few locations, for instance in Wiltshire, Dorset and Devon. The habitats favoured by it have shrunk drastically over the last century, and modern agricultural methods make it difficult to recreate them effectively. I have not often seen them, but they are a delight when they can be found.

A Marsh Fritillary at the nature reserve at Strawberry Banks, Gloucestershire.

A male Marsh Fritillary at Strawberry Banks, a calcareous grassland habitat in Gloucestershire. There has been an alarming decline in numbers of these fritillaries in recent times. The larval food plant is devil's-bit scabious.

Marsh Fritillary

This shrinking beauty is a prophetess –
the wind cannot tear her gossamer wings
as she braves her perils.

Satan himself chewed the end of her scabious,
a healthy root, not scabrous for all that
but still savoury and tasty.

When her kind survive
they dance with danger
as their landscape shrinks – they do not see.

Springtime rains don't scour away
the brightness of their checks and stripes,
chills and cloud can't douse their energy.

But, deprived of damp and bounteous meadows
and friendly sward, they shrink away,
their prophetess foretelling her own fate.

Meadow Brown
Maniola jurtina

The Meadow Brown would be easy to take for granted. It is brown and occurs in meadows, so its name fits. It has a dull colour and a rather weak flight. It occurs in considerable numbers throughout Britain in the high summer, and even keen lepidopterists are prone to ignore it as they search for something more exciting. There are sometimes large numbers in the field next to my Somerset garden. There is one generation and the larvae feed on a range of grasses before overwintering and then pupating in the spring.

The scientific Latin name gave me an idea for the poem. *Maniola* is a diminutive form of the Latin word *manes*, meaning souls or ghosts, in another allusion to the association between butterflies and the spirits of the dead, and thus death itself. During one depressing and rainy day, when any sensible butterfly would have been roosting safely under cover, this name gave rise to the dark thoughts expressed in the poem. The reader must feel free to pass it by if it feels too gloomy and move to a more cheerful one, such as Clouded Yellow.

I am not the only one to have been inspired by the butterfly to artistic expression; Professor Philip Howse (2014) points out that a Meadow Brown with the beak of a bird is pictured

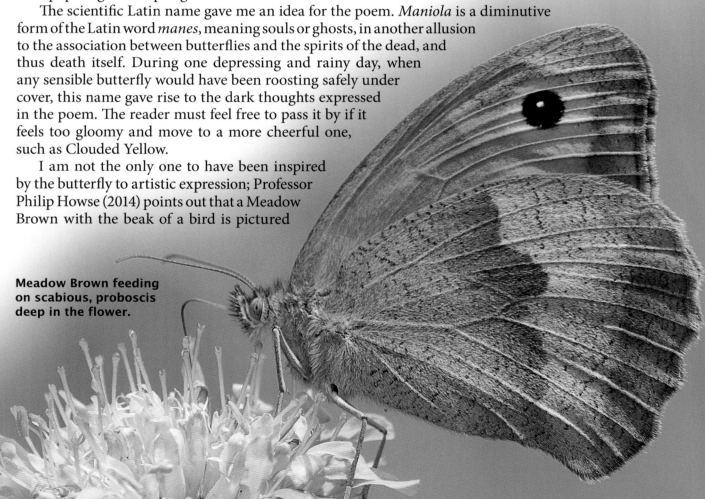

Meadow Brown feeding on scabious, proboscis deep in the flower.

in a triptych by the fifteenth-century painter Hieronymus Bosch, depicting a positively hellish scene. This butterfly is more reassuring than infernal. The butterfly in Yealand's photograph could almost be considered pretty were it not for the fierce competition that the Meadow Brown faces in the beauty contest of the butterfly world.

Jurtina, according to Maitland Emmet (1991), is a non-existent name, and in his view likely to be a misprint for *Juturna*, the name of (yet another!) water-nymph, this time Roman.

Female Meadow Brown. Still a common butterfly, but numbers have declined through the loss of traditional hay meadows.

Meadow Brown

Each day another step towards the void,
the absence of existence, a vacuum,
the great nothingness, not even black
because blackness is something.

It may hurtle towards you
as a speeding unseen train
or a sharp pain in the night,
but it could materialise slowly
as gradual dilapidation
or humiliating shrinkage of age
at the end of a street
in a city gone to seed.

You would not regret the coming
of the bottomless endless chasm,
le néant sans l'être,[1]
if you did not know of it,
if the great inevitable nothing
was an emptiness in the mind,
not even suspected;
but your great gift of knowledge
is also your burden.

The Meadow Brown,
like any other butterfly,
is luckier than you;
though named for souls
of now-departed nymphs
it can't foresee the last flap of its wings,
when brown turns to black
in the final flight to nowhere.

[1]French: 'Nothingness without being', a reference
to the book L'Être et le Néant, by Jean-Paul Sartre.

A female Meadow Brown
warms herself in the
morning sunshine.

Mountain Ringlet
Erebia epiphron

This is another dark-coloured butterfly with a dark name. *Erebia* is from the Greek *Erebos*, the Greek deity of darkness and the name of the tenebrous part of the underworld through which the dead pass on their way to Hades. *Epiphron* means 'thoughtful', the very best of the possible states of mind that anyone passing through Erebos might be expected to possess.

The Mountain Ringlet occurs in this country only in the mountainous regions of the Scottish Highlands and the English Lake District, and it flies for a few weeks in June and July. Even then it is inclined to wait for sunshine. It has one brood, with larvae feeding on mat-grass, and then hibernating in grass tussocks until the spring.

Its range is so restricted that I have so far not been in the right place at the right time to see one in the wild. I did, however, once see a pinned specimen in a collection, and this is what inspired my poem. Such collections, of course, were hugely fashionable in the nineteenth and early twentieth centuries, and those that have survived can provide valuable scientific evidence to modern researchers.

A villanelle is a nineteen-line poetic form consisting of five tercets followed by a quatrain. The first and final lines of the first tercet alternate as the final lines of the succeeding tercets until the last stanza, where they conclude the poem. If you, the reader, find that description of a villanelle difficult to follow, please do not worry. I, the writer, can assure you that writing one is just as difficult. I hope you consider it worth the effort.

**The Mountain Ringlet,
a species occuring only in
Scotland and the English
Lake District above 350
metres.**

The larvae of the Mountain Ringlet
feed at night and hide during the day.

Mountain Ringlet

Villanelle

A Mountain Ringlet's skewered by a pin –
a rarity displayed inside a case,
condemned to perish for an unknown sin.

Who snatched this creature from its nearest kin,
and kept it from the others of its race?
A Mountain Ringlet skewered by a pin.

They might not feel contented in their skin
if with this Ringlet they should change their place,
condemned to perish for an unknown sin.

Collectors may think only they can win
when they encounter coldly face to face
a Mountain Ringlet skewered by a pin.

Still, maybe they have nagging doubts within
for those deprived of dignity and grace,
condemned to perish for an unknown sin.

But even if the killer could unpin
this Ringlet, still it suffered its disgrace:
a Mountain Ringlet skewered by a pin,
condemned to perish for an unknown sin.

Northern Brown Argus

Aricia artaxerxes

Here is a third brown butterfly in a row. This time, though, the poem is rather frivolous. The Northern Brown Argus is a near-relative of the Brown Argus and the two are very similar. The main distinguishing feature is a small black or white spot that is present on the Northern but not on the other. The butterfly in the photograph has white spots. Only a true butterfly devotee would go out of their way to find one of these butterflies. It occurs in Scotland and the far north of England. The larvae feed on common rock-rose and hibernate before pupating in the spring. Adults fly from June until August in one brood.

Ariccia (with two 'c's in modern Italian, instead of one in Latin) is a town near Rome with a very long history. Just for the record it was said to be the home town of the mother of the Roman Emperor Augustus.

Artaxerxes was the name of several emperors of ancient Persia, none of whom, it can safely be assumed, had any connection whatsoever with Scotland. Artaxerxes III was especially ruthless, murdering most of his family in order to gain and then retain his throne. He was rewarded with long life, which does seem rather unfair.

Northern Brown Argus. This one is the Scottish subspecies *artaxerxes* which has the prominent white spot on each forewing. Small populations of the same butterfly (subspecies *salmacis*) exist in a few locations in the north of England. They have a black spot in place of the white.

Northern Brown Argus

Across the desk my head was slumped
– this insect had the poet stumped.
What was there to be said
that's worthy to be read?

But then its spirit gave a sign,
and soon there was a rhyming line:
this Northern Argus race
deserves a special place.

I've never heard this species sing,
nor even seen it on the wing,
but still it calls, though mute,
this brown evasive brute.

Atop its wings it has two spots,
but underneath the usual dots;
it can't be an affliction
if that's its one distinction.

Northern Brown Argus – just visible
is the white spot in the centre of the
underwing which distinguishes the
sub-species *artaxerxes* which inhabits
the Scottish part of its territory.

Orange-tip

Anthocaris cardamines

The name *Anthocaris* combines Greek words for flower and grace. *Cardamines* refers to the bittercress genus of plants, which includes the cuckoo flower, on which Orange-tip females lay their eggs, and which grace their flowers in the process. There is one generation, with adults flying between and April and June. Overwintering is in the pupal stage.

The English name is a precise description of one half of the species – the male – but the females do not have orange-tipped wings. The wings of both sexes, however, are beautifully decorated with yellow and black scales which give an impression of green mottling. They frequent damp meadows, unspoilt open meadows and country streams. I can picture them in my imagination fluttering along a flowery river bank, settling from time to time to mate or feed. They are butterflies that remind us

A female Orange-tip feeding on cuckooflower and showing the pretty green mottling on the underwing.

An Orange-tip resting on flax
displaying the distinctive orange tips
which indicate he's the male of the
species.

Orange-tip

When spring is well unwound
and in full swing,
when Blue tits leave the fat balls
to fill their beaks instead
with twigs and feathers for their nests,
a flame-edged roamer
busies through the archway
from the green beyond,
a flying smile, a live rebuke to darkness.

The Orange-tip monitors
the primrose bank,
his white and burnished copper
faster than the yellow-pale petals
quivering in the breeze,
 and all their colours singing youth.

His green-dappled mate
seeks out cuckoo flower
by the brook.

Both are quickly gone
from corner of the eye
but life is good on a morning
tinged with orange.

that life is still worth living after a dark or cold winter, and can cheer the spirits on a sunny spring day.

The French call this butterfly L'auroré, which roughly means 'infused by the dawn', hinting that the first light of the year has gilded their wings with young light. With its touch of French romance, this is a more evocative name than the English one.

When my son was a boy this was his favourite butterfly because it could be seen on the wing at around the same time as his birthday.

Margaret Fountaine
(1862-1940)

Many people from the leisured classes in nineteenth and early 20th century Britain enjoyed collecting insects, especially butterflies. Some were ordinary people who liked an outdoor hobby, and others were eccentrics who would go to great lengths to secure their prize. Margaret Fountaine was a vicar's daughter and heiress who collected butterflies. She was an unusual woman for her time, but she was far more than this, being a brilliant natural history illustrator and a knowledgeable and respected entomologist, becoming a member of the Linnaean Society and the Royal Entomological Society.

Edited versions of her diaries were published after her death under the titles *Love among the Butterflies* and *Butterflies and Late Loves*. The editing perhaps over-emphasised her adventurous love life and travels and understated her achievements as a scientist in an effort to maximise sales of the books. It is true that she travelled and then lived for some years, in defiance of the conventions of her time, with a married Syrian dragoman (Middle Eastern guide and interpreter), Khalil Neimy, who accompanied her on her butterfly-hunting expeditions. It is also true, though, that her immense collection of butterflies, amassed in the wild places of several continents, was considered of major importance, and her drawings were deemed worthy of display in the London Natural History Museum.

Margaret Fountaine was a remarkable individual who deserves to be remembered for her enormous contribution to the study of butterflies, as well as for her unconventional private life. It is said that when she died on a Trinidad mountain she was still holding a butterfly net.

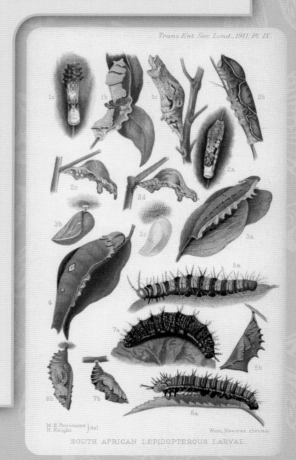

Trans. Ent. Soc. Lond., 1911; Pl. IX.

M. E. Fountaine } del
H. Knight

West, Newman chromo.

SOUTH AFRICAN LEPIDOPTEROUS LARVAE.

Painted Lady
Vanessa cardui

Literary opinion has it that the name Vanessa came from the title of the poem *Cadenus and Vanessa*, written in 1713 by the eighteenth century writer Dean Jonathan Swift, author of *Gulliver's Travels*. He is said to have invented the names so that he could write clandestinely about one of his students, Esther Vanhomrigh, who was also his lover. 'Inappropriate behaviour' in educational institutions is not a twenty-first century invention. Cadenus is an anagram of decanus, meaning 'dean', in other words Swift himself. Vanessa is derived from the first three letters of Esther Vanhomrigh's surname and the first two of her first name. It is not a Latin word; it just resembles one. I wonder how many modern women called Vanessa would realise that it was invented by a Dublin cleric as a nickname for his mistress?

Cardu is from Carduus, meaning 'thistle', which happens to be the food plant in Britain of the larva of this butterfly, although it will feed on some other plants.

The English name is very striking, but, as the poem points out, not all Painted Ladies are Ladies. Curiously, there are some lines in Swift's poem that seem to echo the gender ambiguity of the butterfly in my poem:

Painted Lady resting. This strong flier is often capable of migrating to Britain from north Africa.

Painted Lady

'...The Queen of Learning gravely smiles.
Down from Olympus comes with joy,
Mistakes Vanessa for a boy...'

Vanessa was definitely not a boy, although my Painted Lady is. In case any reader is concerned that I have not allowed for the possibility that my butterfly could have been transgender, non-binary, gender fluid, or have any other contemporary gender preference, please be assured that it would have been equally acceptable. The poem would simply have been rather more complicated and a lot longer.

The Painted Lady is a very adventurous migrant, and can be found almost anywhere in these islands at the right times of the year. It has been spotted even on the island of St Kilda in the Outer Hebrides. Every spring, butterflies leave North Africa and the Middle East, and some of them fly all the way to this country. Others settle in countries along the way, such as Spain or France, and their offspring then migrate northwards to Britain and Ireland. This means, unusually, that it is continuously brooded, but only occasionally overwinters in Britain as an adult. Their numbers vary a lot from year to year according to the weather and conditions in their places of origin. One thing is always true, though: some are ladies and some are gentlemen.

*I am a Painted Lady
with finely coloured cloak;
alas! The One who made me
created me a bloke.*

*It makes things rather awkward
when no-one thinks I'm male –
they cannot get me sorted,
I look too fair and frail.*

*Why should we all be ladies?
It's quite beyond my ken;
We all start off as babies
But some grow up as men.*

*And why should I be "painted"
as if a shameless tart?
I'd rather not be tainted
With such a doubtful art.*

*Those human folk baptized us
and when they chose a name
they did not seem to notice
that we're not all the same.*

*I hope you will remember
one vital thing at least:
I'm muscular and limber –
I am a hunky beast.*

*No pretty dainty girl
with flowery-perfumed scent,
no dresses all a-swirl
I am a Painted Gent.*

Painted Lady or Painted Gentleman?

Peacock
Inachis io

Inachos was a figure of ancient Greek mythology, the first king of Argos and a river god. *Io*, his daughter, was a priestess of Hera in Argos. According to legend she was a mortal, seduced by Zeus, who changed her into a heifer to escape detection, even though, we might imagine, this could have reduced her sex appeal somewhat. Zeus's ever-jealous wife, Hera, found out about the affair, a she usually did, and had Io the heifer guarded by Argus the many-eyed monster, to keep her safe from her lascivious husband. But then Argus was killed by Hermes, who first sent the monster to sleep with a very boring story about Pan and Syrinx. Hera set his eyes in the tail of a peacock. Io, no longer under the watchful eye of a monster, though still a cow, then wandered about for a while, pursued by a rather horrid gadfly. The rest of her story is even more complicated, but she eventually managed to be turned back into a human, marry an Egyptian king, and have children and grandchildren, one of whom had fifty daughters. Not bad for a river god's daughter and temporary cow.

My poem has no connection at all with this story, and was inspired by the passage of the English seasons, and an incident involving a Christmas tree. Peacock butterflies overwinter as hibernating adults, sometimes indoors, and increased warmth or light can tempt them to wake up and fly about in the middle of winter. That is how the incident in the poem occurred. We had a log fire in the dining room and the Christmas dinner scene was ablaze with candles and Christmas tree lights. It caused great astonishment. We did not see where the butterfly went after the incident described in the poem, but I think it likely that it went back to sleep until the spring, when it would have flown out to mate.

Peacock larvae feed on nettle, and after the pupal stage, emerge as adults in midsummer. They can be seen almost anywhere in Britain. The name *Peacock* refers to the spectacular coloured patterns on the butterfly's wings, reminiscent of the eyespots on the wings of the peacock bird.

A newly-hatched Peacock butterfly showing its brilliant colours.

Peacock

The Peacock's sometimes heard before it's seen
in rapid search for blooms, to feed and preen
on long light days when fruitful plenty rules
and insects wander even as the evening cools.

But time moves on, and soon there comes the day
when nectar-flowers of summer fade away:
the Peacock seeks a secret roosting place
in which to hide in peace without a trace,
where freezing gales won't bend its fragile wings
and where it sleeps secure from winter's stings.

At Christmas one such Peacock warmed and stirred
by roaring fires – its wings spread out then whirred
past startled turkey-eaters at their meal
and children uttered a delighted squeal.

It flew among the garlands, settling twice
but launched itself and rushed off in a trice,
then circled closely round the Christmas tree
as if in search of things it could not see.

And so at last it triumphed in its quest:
perched on the fairy's wand, it came to rest,
an unexpected messenger of Spring,
a winter fairy-flower on the wing.

This early-season Peacock with faded
colours and a rather tatty appearance,
indicates that it overwintered as a
butterfly and has emerged to warm
itself in the spring sunshine.

Pearl-bordered Fritillary
Boloria euphrosyne

The Pearl-bordered Fritillary is the more rare 'big sister' of the Small Pearl-bordered Fritillary which also appears in this book. She is just as beautiful, and her wings are decorated with silver 'pearls' on their underside. The name 'Fritillary' has been explained in the section about the Dark Green Fritillary.

This Fritillary has a single brood and flies between May and July in woodland clearings and grasslands in isolated colonies scattered across the British Isles. I have seen specimens on Dartmoor. The larvae feed on violets and after hibernating continue to feed until they pupate. They emerge from late April onwards. Because of habitat loss it is unfortunately one of our most threatened species.

Boloria is believed to be from the Greek word for 'fishing net', applied to the butterfly because of the chequered wing patterns. *Euphrosyne* was one of the three Charites, or Graces, representing fun, merriment and joy, and was the personification of elegance and beauty. Thalia was another of the Graces – see Heath Fritillary. They were some of the many daughters of Zeus, and were said to have come into the world in order to provide moments of pleasure and goodwill. Finding a lovely Pearl-bordered Fritillary in the world is guaranteed to give more than a moment of pleasure.

One of the earliest of the fritillaries to emerge, in late April and early May, the Pearl-bordered has declined in numbers by 71% since 1976.

A Pearl-bordered Fritillary warms itself in the morning sun. The caterpillar feeds on species of violet.

When I was writing the poem I wondered where the butterfly's pearls might have originated. I then found that pearls are closely associated with dragons in Chinese folklore. They have them on their scales, and an old tale recounts that when a blue dragon and a yellow dragon fight one another in the clouds, fireballs and pearls fall to the ground. For the rest of the story, please read the poem.

Chinese mythology also relates a sad tale about butterflies, in the tale of Zhu and Liang, known as the 'butterfly lovers'. Zhu Yingtai was a young woman from a wealthy family whose love for a young man she met during her studies was thwarted by her parents, who considered him unsuitable. It is a long and melancholy story; the lovers were eventually united in death but they emerged from their shared grave as two butterflies and flew away. The butterfly lovers could then be together. The notion of butterflies as spirits seems to be almost universal in human cultures, and must go back a long way in our history.

Pearl-bordered Fritillary

Boloria euphrosyne sports the finest wings
all strung with crescent pearls;
she dances over violets where she drapes her gems
on the birthing places of her young.

The nursery flowers are caressed by springtime showers
and from the rains come, so they say,
the nacreous gems that ring the butterfly wings,
confected and scattered by violence in the skies.

Why dragons fight we cannot know,
but maybe over gold, or massive appetites,
or which has won the right to swallow the sun,
or maybe just for writhing serpent fun.

But from this conflict in the pillars of storms
come pearls that fall down with the rains;
the dragons chance to irrigate
and in a fiery breath illuminate Fritillary wings.

Purple Emperor
Apatura iris

The English name for the Purple Emperor seems to have been invented in the eighteenth century, in honour of this magnificent creature cloaked in imperial purple, the traditional colour of authority since ancient times. Despite being only the second largest British butterfly (the Swallowtail is the largest) it is widely regarded as our premier butterfly. Anyone who has spotted one gorging on the juices of rotting animal carcases or fox turds may wonder why.

It has one brood, flying from late June to mid August. The larvae feed on willow leaves, and hibernate while small. They carry on feeding in the spring and then pupate underneath leaves. Only the male adult has a purple sheen on its upperwings.

Apatura may be a corruption of 'Apaturia', which were ancient Greek festivals held annually in Ionian towns. A more likely derivation, though, is from a Greek word meaning 'to deceive', since the colours of the upper wings of this butterfly can appear to change deceptively from dark grey to purple, depending on the angle of view.

Iris was a demi-goddess of Greek mythology, appearing in the form of a rainbow as a messenger from the gods. With its colourful wings shimmering in the sunshine, the Purple Emperor is a worthy bearer of this name.

Matthew Oates, author of *In Pursuit of Butterflies,* has spent a lifetime studying the Purple Emperor and is a leading expert on this magnificent creature. As I write he is working on his forthcoming book, *His Imperial Majesty: A Natural History of the Purple Emperor Butterfly*, due to be published by Bloomsbury in the summer of 2020. He also writes a blog entitled 'The Purple Empire'.

My first sighting of these butterflies was in a forest in central France. The habitat seemed perfect, and a local guide book suggested that Emperors might be found in the vicinity. Something has to be used to tempt Emperors down from tree tops, where they feed on honeydew a long way above ground level. I had read about their penchant for rotten meat, but did not have any with me, so I wondered whether rotten fish might do just as well. I left some elderly sardines in the sun for a while until they were thoroughly putrefying and then scattered them at one end of a car park near to some suitable trees. Sure enough, some hungry Emperors soon swooped down to feed, much to my pleasure. They were not the only ones to notice these errant sardines, many miles from the nearest sea coast. I heard an astonished French hiker calling out, in French: 'Look, Henry, some fish, why on earth are *they* there – it's not a beach!'

Although my poem bemoans the threat posed by tree felling and urban sprawl, in fact the Purple Emperor has been holding its own in recent years thanks to some effective conservation work by its ecological royal subjects, including Matthew Oates.

The effect of light on wing scales: one wing on this male Purple Emperor shimmers purple, the other does not. Females are a little larger and with a deep brown background colour throughout.

Purple Emperor

The realm above the broad-spread oaks
is an anarchy of Emperors
governed by rules, and no rulers
but the tidal pull of the seasons;
Emperors temporal and powerless
commanding only their scintillant wings.

Despots of the honeydew, tyrants of the flowers
these denizens of high society
suffer no virtues, enjoy no vice
though the royal standards lapse
when they suck at fewmets for a meal
or embrace the nidorous noisome
temptation of naturalist's meat.

These Emperors do not crave blood
on vainglorious battlefields
arrest history with railway timetables
fail in overzealous duty
bestowed absolutely by God:
these sovereigns succeed not and fail not.

If Bonaparte had sported purple
rather than the tricolore
St Helena would still be obscure;
if Nicholas had been the purple Czar
of all the Russias,
Lenin would never
have had the chance to murder
by squeamish proxy one Ekaterinburg night.

In a world within a world
every one luxuriates, exults
in the imperium over the trees
free and equal, incorruptible;
but even if the fellers of the woods
spare these elusive Emperors,
foul fumes and concrete blocks
could quietly dethrone them.

**The Purple Emperor's underwing
– beautiful but not purple.**

Purple Hairstreak

Neozephyrus quercus

Adult Purple Hairstreaks also spend a lot of their time perched on the tops of oak trees drinking honeydew, the sticky sugary fluid secreted by aphids after feeding on plant sap. This is the adult's main food. When I discovered this I was immediately reminded of Tennyson's poem, *The Lotos-Eaters*, and so in my own poem I have written about the 'honeydew-drinkers'. In Greek mythology the lotus-eaters, as suggested by the name, were people who ate the lotus plant. The fruits and flowers had a narcotic effect, and the lotus-eaters lived in a perpetual blissful daze. Tennyson, in turn, describes a group of mariners who, on eating the lotos (his spelling), are put into an altered dreamy state and isolated from the outside world. The Purple Hairstreak is the 'lotus-eater' of the butterfly world, and I have imagined it has an untroubled existence on the oak canopy.

They can be found almost anywhere that oaks grow in sufficient numbers, even in city parks. They have one generation and fly between July and September, overwintering as developing larvae inside their eggs to

A female Purple Hairstreak showing patches of iridescent blue/purple on the forewings. Her male partner will have a more even sheen across his wings.

hatch in the spring. Males have more purple colouring than females.

The English name accurately describes their purple colouring. The *quercus* part of the scientific Latin name correctly identifies the food plant of Purple Hairstreak larvae, as *quercus* means 'oak' in Latin. Zephyrus was the Greek god of the west wind. Like many of his fellow deities he had a complicated love life. For a while he was madly in love with Hyacinthus, a very beautiful Spartan youth. When another god ran off with Hyacinthus, Zephyrus was peevish and jealous and caused the object of his affections to be killed. After that he is said to have started showing an interest in women. It is not clear why Zephyrus would be associated with Purple Hairstreaks, but it is no doubt windy from time to time at the top of oak trees, and Zephyrus is a gentle wind, not so strong as to blow the butterflies off their high perches.

Purple Hairstreak

High on their glistening purple towers
in their perpetual afternoon
where each moment is a never-changing age
aloft they sit and sip,
nor ever fold their wings, and rarely wander far:
they are the drinkers of the honeyed honeydew,
sweet sustenance for these leisured beings.

The Hairstreaks feed on quirky Quercus oaks,
content and languid,
with only the sky above and a leaf below;
they are not escaping from mountainous seas
or a wandering life in foreign ports;
they are not tired of the always-rocking waves.

They just enjoy the swaying branches of the trees
on a higher gentler plane,
addicted to calm reflection of the violet blue.
They are the honeydew drinkers,
quirkiest of them all.

Resting on bracken, this Purple
Hairstreak has come down briefly
from her life high in the oak canopy.
Although rarely seen Purple Hairstreaks
are in fact the commonest of the
Hairstreak family.

Red Admiral
Vanessa atalanta

This is another migrant butterfly of the *Vanessa* sub-family (see Painted Lady, for the origin of this name), and they have a continuous life cycle that allows them to overwinter as larvae or adults. It used to be thought that Red Admirals were unable to survive British winters. In recent times, though, many have been found to overwinter successfully, perhaps because of milder winters. I have personally witnessed this, having discovered a live specimen just waking up one spring in Cornwall. My poem was written some time ago when it was still widely supposed that they would all die of cold. Sadly, however, many of them still do die during hibernation.

Atalanta was another mythical Greek lady with a remarkable career. Abandoned by her parents when she was born, she was raised by a she-bear and became a very fast runner. She hunted mythical boars and shot and killed centaurs that tried to rape her. She was prepared to marry only a man who could beat her in a foot-race, and killed all who tried and failed. Melanion eventually became her husband, having beaten her in a race by dropping in her path golden apples, given to him by Aphrodite, which delayed her as she stopped to pick them up. She may have sailed with the Argonauts (see above also), and ended up by being changed into a leopard by Zeus, after which she may have remained beautiful but marital life would have become hazardous for her husband.

The English name, Admiral, is believed to be a corruption of the original Victorian name Admirable. The only nautical connection for the Red Admiral is that many of the specimens in the British Isles have to migrate over the sea. According to Korean folklore red butterflies are the bringers of danger or evil, but for me their striking scarlet and black wings are magnificent, and they are one of my favourites.

The Red Admiral seldom manages to survive the British winter, so most of those we see are the result of successive waves of migrants from continental Europe.

Red Admiral

The admirable red is tricked
to fly on tempting southern breeze
where common sense and whim conflict,
beset by threat it never sees.

Its scarlet black and velvet coat
avoids the touch of human hand;
it flaunts itself yet stays remote –
a royal in a foreign land.

It feasts and gorges on the flowers
of English summer, greed unstilled
as it voraciously devours
the sweet rain by the sun distilled.

But this indulgence has an aim:
Vanessa Atalanta tries
to fortify its brittle frame
for living in its winter guise.

As nights close in it starts the quest
for sanctuary in winter time
to keep its sleeping wings at rest,
away from gales and lethal rime.

It hibernates without a breath
in colours fit for queen or king,
but overcome by peaceful death
the Admiral never sees the spring.

With wings closed and forewing hidden the Red Admiral suddenly becomes wonderfully camouflaged, blending in perfectly against its surroundings such as a log or a gravel path. Here the butterfly rests on its preferred choice of food plant, the common nettle.

Ringlet
Aphantopus hyperantus

This poem, frankly, is light and utterly trivial, and is the result of a challenge from an old school friend to write my first butterfly limerick, so I wrote three limericks joined together.

The Ringlet is a widespread butterfly, flying as one generation from June to August in damp grassy places, quite often in large colonies. The larvae eat various grasses and overwinter in that form. The sexes are similar to one another.

The English name must have been given because of the small rings that are visible underneath its hindwing. *Aphantopus* roughly means 'invisible foot', and alludes to a shrunken foreleg that is characteristic of the species.

Hyperantus was one of the fifty sons (pity his wife!) of Aegyptus, king of Egypt. The twin brother of Aegyptus, Danaus, had fifty daughters, and Aegyptus commanded his sons to marry their cousins. Danaus was not happy with this idea and gave each of his daughters a dagger with which to kill her husband on their wedding night. Forty-nine of the daughters carried out the instruction, leaving just one of the men alive.

As far as I am aware kittens did not play much part in Greek mythology, although people were occasionally turned into cats as a punishment. To my mind this would have been more like a reward, as the life of a cat involves plenty of food, self-indulgence, long naps and pampering from a besotted owner, with only occasional light work chasing mice.

Allowing for murderous kittens of the kind that appear in my poem, Ringlets can be seen widely in the British countryside during the high summer.

Above: Ringlets mating on hawthorn. They will stay together for about 30 minutes before the female flies away to lay her eggs on grass stems. The eggs then fall to the ground where they rest for about 3 weeks until the larvae hatch and seek their preferred coarse grass food plants.

Ringlet

A beautiful Ringlet was smitten
with love for a pretty young kitten.
When he tried to attract her
by landing beside her
he nearly got pounced on and bitten.

'Do you really imagine,' said she,
'that a handsome young pussy like me
could be charmed by a fly?
I'm surprised you would try.'
And at that he attempted to flee.

Alas for the Ringlet, too late,
as the kitten had no wish to wait –
she leapt from a height,
took an open-mouthed bite,
and sealed the poor butterfly's fate.

The Ringlet seeks partial shade. Early morning is a good time to see it, warming itself on bracken fronds. It is one of the UK species that is doing well.

Scotch Argus
Erebia aethiops

For the Argus name, please see 'Brown Argus'. This is a *Scotch* Argus, so called because it flies mainly in Scotland, although it also occurs widely in Europe, Turkey and as far away as Siberia. No doubt the lepidopterists of those countries would like to think that their local specimens are Turkish or Siberian. Much to my regret, I still have not seen one, not even in Siberia. A few brave individuals make it over the border from Scotland into England. The butterfly in my poem is one such interloper.

Scotch Arguses have one brood and fly from July to September. The larvae feed mainly on purple moor-grass and then hibernate until the spring in grass tussocks. It is not in the same butterfly family as the Brown Argus, but it is a relative of the Mountain Ringlet, and so they share the first part of the scientific Latin name, *Erebus*, the Greek deity of darkness. This god acquires a mildly exotic connection with Africa through the second part of the name, *aethiops*, which refers to Ethiopia, a country of mainly dark-skinned people. These names seem curiously incongruous for a butterfly that frequents the peaty bogs, heather-clad mountainsides and woodland clearings of the Scottish Highlands. What would a traveller from Addis Ababa make of these habitats, and would they enjoy the drizzle and the porridge?

Besides, the butterfly in my poem is not Scottish but English.

The Scotch Argus flourishes in areas damp grassland where scattered shrubs and trees offer some shelter. Its food plant is usually, but not exclusively, purple moor-grass. It is most prolific in northern and western parts of Scotland, but can also be found in certain locations in Cumbria.

Scotch Argus

I am the dark exotic seeking light,
a handsome Ethiopian shining bright
on chilly moors that Africans might shun,
yet I explore them willingly for fun.

And if I'd travelled up from Erebus,
perhaps against the odds, ceteris paribus,[2]
the dark and brooding Scottish heights
would shine with brilliant Northern lights.

I am an Argus, yes, but there's a catch:
this Argus is pretending. I'm not Scotch.
I live across the border, live a lie,
a Scotch in England, proud. I shall not hide.

[2] *Latin for 'other things being equal'.*

Silver-spotted Skipper
Hesperia comma

In Greek mythology *Hesperia* was one of the nymphs of the evening who guarded the golden apples in the western garden of Hera, Zeus's wife. The apples could impart immortality when eaten but, like the forbidden fruit of the Garden of Eden, could be consumed only with the permission of the deity. As Hera believed that she could not trust even the beautiful and virtuous Hesperides nymphs to resist the temptation to have an illicit fruit snack, she also installed Ladon the dragon to look over them. He was immortal, had one hundred heads and never slept, and so was hardly a relaxing companion for those poor girls.

In the legends Hera's garden was often placed in Iberia, possibly in what is now southern Portugal, close to the 'encircling sea', as the Atlantic was known in the days before the American continents were known to the inhabitants of the Mediterranean region.

Silver spots clearly visible on the underside of this Silver-spotted Skipper.

131

This species has been increasing in numbers and extending its range since the 1970s. Warmer years, the recovery of rabbits (after myxomatosis) and better sheep and cattle grazing regimes on chalk and limestone grasslands – these are among the reasons given for its growing population.

Part of the Silver-Spotted Skipper's scientific name is 'comma'. The word 'comma' in Ancient Greek signified a pause in text or speech. In modern English it is a punctuation mark. The name may have been applied to this butterfly with reference to the underwing silver marks, some of which resemble commas. Rather confusingly it is not related to the butterfly that bears the name 'Comma' in English. They belong to different butterfly families.

For a similar reason the name of the butterfly is 'silver-spotted'. Like the other Skippers, Silver-Spotted Skippers have an energetic whirring flight that no doubt gave them their name. These skippers became quite scarce but have recovered somewhat recently, and in the UK are found only in southern England. I have seen them in Dorset, at Fontmell Down on a rather steep flowery slope, where you are in danger of sliding down the hill as you chase after a very active butterfly. The pleasure of seeing such a rarity more or less compensated for having my wallet stolen from the car that afternoon. Sheep's-fescue is the larval food plant, and there is one brood, with adults flying in the high summer. Eggs laid at this time do not hatch until the spring.

Silver-spotted Skipper

Hidden in the fescue grass
a lead and platinum sheath-case
edged with gold
lies warm, inert but live
alert to an esoteric sign
for sudden stirring.

At first, the slightest quiver,
vibration of a shivering feather,
then a gentle quaking of the blades above
that tears the shiny vessel.

Streaks of light give added strength,
a budge, a heave:
nature's Fabergé cleft apart.

But from its womb
erupts a crumpled, folded creature of the air,
still without wings.

Microscopic pulses fill the veins
until new willing wings
are dried transparent in the sun.

A flicker, and the new-born surfs the breeze
in search of nectar-drinks
from dwarfish thistle clumps.

Vladimir Nabokov
(1899-1977)

Vladimir Nabokov is best known as a novelist, author of *Lolita* and *Pale Fire*. But he was also a poet, critic, university teacher, nature artist and distinguished entomologist with a passionate interest in butterflies. Some would say that he was a polymathic genius.

His early life was not easy. When he was still a teenager his family was forced to flee the Russian Revolution. He was brainy, however, and studied literature at Cambridge University as well as living for some time in Germany and France. Later on, since his Jewish wife was in danger from the rise of the murderously anti-semitic Nazi regime, Nabokov moved with her to the United States, only returning to Europe some years after the end of the Second World War.

Few of the readers of his best-selling books in his lifetime are likely to have known that he was also the curator of lepidoptera (butterflies and moths) at the Museum of Comparative Zoology at Harvard University. He collected and documented hundreds of butterfly species and made beautiful drawings of many of them. Although he was largely self-taught, he became an acknowledged expert.

Nabokov specialised in the *Lycaenidae* butterflies (Blues, Coppers and Hairstreaks). In 1943 he found and named the Karner Blue butterfly (*Plebejus melissa samuelis*), a distant relative of the Silver-Studded Blue that occurs in Britain. He was so pleased with his discovery that he wrote a poem about it: *On Discovering a Butterfly*. Here are just a few lines from it:

> *'I found it and I named it, being versed*
> *in taxonomic Latin; thus became*
> *godfather to an insect and its first*
> *describer — and I want no other fame.'*

He expressed a theory during his lifetime, based on study of their genitalia, that *Polyommatus* Blues had arrived in the Americas from Asia in waves of migrations, lasting millions of years, when the climate was still warm enough for them to do so across the Bering Strait.

It seems that scientists did not take Nabokov's ideas seriously during his lifetime. Remarkably, though, recent research based on gene-sequencing technology has validated Nabokov's theory. An article in *The Proceedings of the Royal Society of London* showed that he had been right all along. Poetic justice perhaps?

Silver-studded Blue
Plebeius argus

Plebeius is the Latin for 'plebeian', a common person of unrefined and coarse manners. We have met *Argus* before. The Silver-studded Blue has its name because of the small eye-spots on the underside of its wings. It does seem that all of the possible identities of Argus – many-eyed monster guard of an errant heifer, shipbuilder, dog or local newspaper – are at the lower end of the social scale and might feel uncomfortable at lunch in a London West End Club. So it appears quite natural that he or she might be a pleb.

On the other hand, Silver-studded Blue butterflies are anything but common or coarse. Their silvery-blue wings with metallic spots are exquisite and it is well worth crawling down on prickly heathland to look closely. They can be seen at Studland in Dorset, among other places. My wife visited there some years ago with a female friend, and saw some butterflies. But they also got more than they bargained for when they accidentally wandered onto the gay naturist beach. They told me that the experience was mind-broadening but not necessarily uplifting.

Despite their relative rarity, with a range restricted mainly to southern England, these butterflies can sometimes be seen locally in great numbers, as has sometimes been the case at its most northerly recorded sight in Shropshire.

A male Silver-studded Blue – a heathland butterfly now found largely in southern England and on coastal dunes in Cornwall and a few sites in north Wales and Pembrokeshire.

135

Silver-studded Blues mating – the male is on the right, showing the more prominent light blue reflective scales. The female (left) shows the 'silver studs' on the outer edge of the hindwing.

Silver-studded Blue

Thank goodness
I do not have to run
the length of cold and muddy
public school England
or wait in the rain for a bus
that does not come
or arrive much too early for the dentist.

Thank goodness
I am not (yet) in a hospital bed
with a swollen face and empty stomach
as I count the railway wagons pass
on the viaduct outside.

Thank goodness
I am not standing
next to an elderly banker with bad breath
on the 7 a.m. to Waterloo,
or lying awake
the night before leaving my wife.

Thank goodness
I am not walking towards
a French car, its wheels still spinning in the air
with two old peasants
hanging upside down inside by their seat belts
too shocked to speak.

They have one brood, and the adults fly in June to August, depending on where they are. The larvae can feed on heathers, but also on rock-rose and bird's-foot trefoil. They overwinter as eggs.

The poem is more about the brightening effect on human spirits of finding butterflies as beautiful as this one, than it is about the butterfly itself. In case the reader should wonder, all of the experiences mentioned in the poem are based on episodes in my own life.

Thank goodness I found my wallet
under the bed after two days of panic,
and I didn't by mistake board the plane to Kabul
instead of the flight to Venice.

And, thank goodness, instead,
I can watch the Silver-Studded Blue
under a silver blue sky
for a perfect sliver of time,
and all is warmth and peace.

Silver-washed Fritillary

Argynnis paphia

These are quite large butterflies, and glide elegantly in woodland glades, mainly in southern England and Wales. They pass the winter as larvae, which feed on violets in the spring and then pupate. The adults fly from June to August in one brood. Females are paler than males, with larger dark spots, whereas males have black streaks, or sex brands, on their forewings. A small proportion of the females appear in a bronze-green variation, with the scientific name *Valezina*. The celebrated lepidopterist and wildlife illustrator, Frederick William Frohawk, (1861-1946), was so taken with the beauty of the *Valezina* rarity that he gave his own daughter the same name. She became Viscountess Bolingbroke, and in 1996 inaugurated a commemorative sign marking the 'Frohawk Ride' in the New Forest.

Argynnis is one of the names for Aphrodite, the ancient Greek goddess of love and beauty. She had many incarnations, or rather, as she was a goddess, deifications. *Paphia* refers to Paphos, the Cypriot coastal town and her reputed birthplace. Pygmalion, the mythical sculptor, created a statue of Aphrodite and then fell in love with it. This was perhaps the mythological equivalent of falling in love with a present-day inflatable doll, or a robot. Anyway, Pygmalion was in luck, because the spiritual presence of the goddess entered into his statue, which became the living Galatea. In due course she bore Pygmalion a son, Paphos, who gave his name to the city.

The name Silver-Washed refers to the splendid colouring of the underwings – perhaps almost as beautiful as Aphrodite herself. Like other Fritillary butterflies this one has a special relationship with violets, as the larvae feed on them.

The name *Fritillary* is also borne by a family of wild flowers, of which one of the best known in Britain is the Snakeshead Fritillary, in folklore seen as rather sinister. I have never seen them in this light.

My poem is pure fantasy.

The largest of the UK's fritillaries, the Silver-washed in this photo shows the silver streaks across its underwing which have given rise to its name.

Silver-washed Fritillary

There come messengers from Paphos,
amber gold green shining and pink –
climbing high over ancient trees
and sliding waterways.

They could bear love spells or potions
to masquerade as pheromones;
they could perhaps be stretching time
to give pining lovers longer
to enjoy their exquisite pain.

They glide in private finery
and hide their secret purposes:
they glisten still with the spray
from the shining fountains of the goddess.

But if these strange contingencies
seem too worldly or banal
the truth is nothing so prosaic;
Venus has sent them for violets
to decorate her flaxen hair.

The Silver-washed Fritillary is a fast, strong flier spending time flying high among deciduous woodland trees (where it feeds on aphid honeydew) and descending to feed further on brambles and thistles. It lays its eggs in crevices of oak bark where the larvae overwinter before descending in the spring to seek out their food plant, dog-violets. The strong, parallel dark lines on the forewings are its sex brands.

Small Blue
Cupido minimus

The Small Blue lives in small scattered colonies on dry sheltered grasslands and embankments. The larvae feed on kidney vetch, and sometimes each other, and there are two southerly flight periods in May to June and July to August, but only one further north. They overwinter as larvae.

Many butterfly names are charming, but this is especially so. *Cupido* was the son of Venus, the Roman name for Aphrodite. The classical myth relates that Venus was jealous of the beauty of the human Psyche, so she sent her own son to try to cause her to fall in love with an ugly monster. The mission failed because Cupid fell in love with Psyche himself, and she with him. He took her to his celestial palace, where he warned her not to look at him, and visited her in the dark, for fear of attracting the anger of Venus. She began to fear that the lover who came to her every night, but whom she could not see, was indeed an ugly monster. So she lit their room with a lamp after Cupid was asleep, hoping to see him, and found that he was in fact very beautiful, but when he woke he abandoned her to the mercies of Venus, who put Psyche into an enchanted sleep. Cupid still loved her, though, and eventually woke her and granted her immortality so that they could be

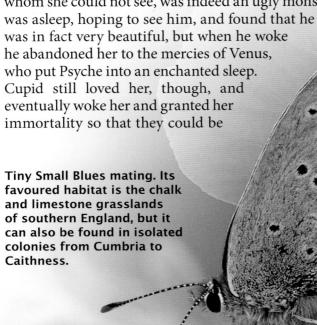

Tiny Small Blues mating. Its favoured habitat is the chalk and limestone grasslands of southern England, but it can also be found in isolated colonies from Cumbria to Caithness.

married. This was, of course, in the days before Civil Partnerships, which might have been more convenient for them. The story is often seen by modern interpreters as an allegory of love overcoming death.

Psyche is also the Ancient Greek word for soul and, by happy coincidence, for butterfly. *Cupido* is traditionally depicted in art as a winged cherub carrying a bow and arrow to fire love-darts. In this case he is *minimus* because the Small Blue butterfly is tiny – scarcely larger than a thumbnail.

It is called a Small Blue because it is small and blue. Quite simple. When newly emerged, Small Blue males have a bluish tinge, but they soon lose scales and turn grey.

Small Blue

Cupido Minimus in the book
is small enough to overlook
and in the field
is well concealed
it's a shy
little fly
a dullish hue
of muddy blue
a twinkle in its eye
and winking antennae
it indulges in
minimal cupidity:
a monstrous meal –
a tiny nectar drop
would perch atop
a pinhead
large enough
for minute angels
to light on
take flight from
like a new small blue.

The male (pictured here) is the more colourful of the sexes – largely grey-black with a dusting of blue on the upperwings. The females are brown, with little or no blue.

Small Copper
Lycaena phlaeas

The Small Copper is an energetic little creature that can appear almost anywhere in the British Isles in the summer. I occasionally see them in my Somerset garden. One of my favourite places to spot them is a coast path in north Cornwall that leads down to Lundy Cove, a little way north of Pentire Head. There is a small ridge of land between the footpath and the cliff edge that is Small Copper territory, where they bask in the Cornish sun and feed on wild thyme flowers. Like so many butterflies, however, even though widespread they are becoming more rare everywhere.

It has two or three generations, depending on geography, and overwinters as a larva, which feeds on sorrel. The pupae are thought to be tended by ants.

The Lycaenid butterflies are a large worldwide family of butterflies of many different colours, of which this little butterfly is a member. The origin of the name *Lycaena* is obscure, but may be a reference to *Lycaea* which, in Greek mythology, was a mountain sacred to Zeus. Alternatively it could be the god Apollo in his guise of wolf-guardian, or an Arcadian shepherd. *Phlaeas* seems to be an invented word. I like to think that it might have been inspired by 'phloginos', meaning a 'flame-coloured gem', that appears in Pliny's *Natural History*, because that is exactly what this butterfly is – a flame-coloured gem.

The English name is altogether more prosaic. The behaviour of the butterfly, though, is quite aggressive, as it will fly up to intercept virtually any passing butterfly, presumably in the hope of finding a mate, or just to have fun. It almost always then returns to the very same spot from which it launched itself. This behaviour prompted the poem.

With as many as three broods in one season, the Small Copper may be seen from May to October. It's a sun-loving butterfly which is susceptible to long periods of the cold and wet.

Small Copper

Fighting Spartan of the glade
bearing double burnished blade
scares its enemy away,
war-like in its fierce display.

Wasps and moths and hoverflies
- all are driven from the skies;
battle joined and bravely won
Phlaeas settles in the sun.

Warriors keep their spirits high,
so, as seasoned fighters say,
small coppers never die -
they only fly away…

Small Copper preparing for battle! When two males cross each other's path they will embark on a fast and furious dog-fight until the intruder returns to its own territory.

Small Heath
Coenonympha pamphilus

When butterfly enthusiasts are out for a butterfly-spotting expedition in the countryside hoping to find exciting rarities such as Fritillaries or Hairstreaks, they may find themselves stumbling through the undergrowth only to find that they have spotted a Small Heath. This butterfly pops up everywhere from April to October, and more often than not will prompt a cry of, 'Oh, it's only a Small Heath, but I suppose it's better than nothing.'

Unusually, there are variable numbers of broods and flight periods. The larvae feed on grasses, and overwinter at different stages of development. Their favourite habitats are dry grasslands such as heathlands.

It is a close relative of the much more rare Large Heath and they share the first part of their scientific Latin name, *Coenonympha*. Some sources say that *Pamphilus* was another of the ill-fated sons of Aegyptus (see 'Ringlet'), although not the one survivor of the murderous brides (that was Lynceus), but he may also have been any one of several theologians, saints and librarians from ancient times.

When Small Heath butterflies settle they always keep

On landing on a flower or grass the Small Heath will usually display the 'eye' on its forewing as a distraction to any bird that might be chasing it. Later, if the weather turns dull or cold, it will lower its forewings taking on the appearance of a dead leaf.

The Small Heath can be found pretty much all over the UK and Ireland in a variety of grassland habitats. It has declined in abundance in southern England but has significantly increased its population in Scotland in recent years.

their wings closed, so the upper side can only be glimpsed very briefly when it is in flight or on landing and take-off. They can be seen in open grassy sites, but seldom on intensively cultivated farmland. Like most butterflies, they prefer wild places.

In Yealand's fine photograph the 'eye-spot' on its forewing is clearly visible, probably acting as a decoy attraction to predatory birds. A hungry peck at the edge of the wing would be unlikely to be fatal, whereas losing the head would be. Butterfly spotters sometimes find surviving specimens with beak-shaped gashes in their forewings. When there is not a perceived risk from bird attack the forewing can be retracted behind the hindwing and the eye-spot is no longer visible.

As the Small Heath is often regarded as dull, boring and inconspicuous I felt that it deserved a specially appreciative sonnet in this book.

Small Heath

Sonnet

To be so plain is wonderful indeed;
a special dullness makes this insect seem
the flying cousin of a common weed –
the kind that nature holds in low esteem.

So shy she hides her upper side from view
and keeps the lower face towards the sun,
although the upper has a brighter hue,
in almost wilful self-denial of fun.

Yet in the fields all kinds of colour abound
inviting exhibition and display,
with summer parties all around,
while wayward Coenonympha stays away;
she holds herself aslant, this coy Small Heath,
concealing secret finery beneath.

When at rest the Small Heath seldom exposes its upperwings which are pale brown, giving the butterfly a lighter appearance in flight than its underwings might suggest.

Small Pearl-bordered Fritillary

Boloria selene

The Small Pearl-bordered Fritillary is only slightly smaller than its big sister the Pearl-bordered, and in any case it is unlikely that this butterfly is psychologically damaged by bearing the name 'small', but I felt for it none the less when I wrote my verses.

Its larvae feed on violets, and there is usually one brood, or occasionally two in the south, with adults on the wing at different periods between April and August, depending on where in the country they emerge. They can be found in various habitats, including scrubby grassland, the edges of woodland, and moorland, as long as there are plenty of violets at the right time. I have spotted them on disused mine workings near Cheddar in Somerset. They hibernate as larvae. They are much more common in Wales and Scotland than in England. Males tend to be a little smaller than females.

The name *Boloria* is apparently from the Greek word meaning 'fishing-net', applied to this butterfly because of the chequered wing patterns. *Selene*, though, was a moon-goddess, the queen of the night who rode her chariot across the heavens, and goddess of magicians. Like many of the deities of ancient Greece she was believed to have pursued a very active love life, and to have had children by a number of fathers. Her most celebrated affair was perhaps with the mortal Endymion. She fell in love with him and put him to sleep for ever so that she might visit him every night. In some versions of the story she is said to be the mother of his fifty sons. By all accounts she was beautiful, like the butterfly named after her. Selene and her chariot were depicted in marbles once part of the stonework of the Parthenon in Athens.

The English name is much more straightforward. See page 35 for 'Fritillary'. You only need to look underneath the stunning wings of this butterfly to see why it is called 'pearl-bordered'.

The Small Pearl-bordered sometimes flies alongside its cousin the Pearl-bordered Fritillary (see page 113). It emerges 2 or 3 weeks later, so it may appear the rather brighter of the two.

Small Pearl-bordered Fritillary

Forever younger siblings of the pearl
the small pearl-bordered butterflies unfurl
competing wings in full view of the sun
because their rivalry is never done.

If the small were smaller, it might be fair
but she is not; the name is hard to bear –
big sister must be better, even prettier,
more attractive, popular and wittier.

But in a contest over body shape,
examined, tested with a measuring tape,
then neither pearl could ever win the prize
because they're more or less an equal size.

To human eyes the two are beautiful,
so making the debate unfruitful:
until the end of life, the final fall,
the 'smaller' one will be forever small.

The small pearls can be seen running along the edge of the hindwing. This specimen is resting in the cool of morning – a good time to spot them on grass stems and bracken.

Small Skipper
Thymelicus sylvestris

There are seven other Skippers in this book, so this is a large family. Some of them are very rare, but the Small Skipper is one of the few British butterflies that seem to have extended their range and abundance. It is a quintessential Skipper and, though small, catches the eye and affection of lepidopterists.

They have just one generation each year, with adults flying between June and September, and can be seen in many parts of England and Wales in grassy places such as road verges or woodland rides. Larvae hibernate as soon as they hatch from their eggs, having eaten their own egg cases, and then pupate in the spring.

It is a butterfly that I see from time in my rural garden, part of which lies right next to a field of mixed grasses grown for hay, and beyond that some mature deciduous woodland. I think it highly likely that the food plant of the Small Skipper caterpillar, a grass known as Yorkshire fog, grows somewhere in the vicinity. It is a grass that occurs very widely in this country, and is not confined to the foggy north, despite its name.

The name *Thymelicus* is shared with the Essex Skipper and in Latin means 'theatrical', in a possible reference to the dramatic and energetic flight of the butterflies. *Sylvestris* means 'of woodland' in Latin. Small Skippers do not typically live in woods, so this part of the name does not fit, even though it sounds attractive.

Small Skippers are actually larger than several other Skippers such as the Lulworth, Grizzled and Essex (which it very closely resembles).

Small Skippers are territorial and fast, nimble fliers which make them difficult to follow through the rough grasses. The photo shows clearly the angled position of the wings which is typical of the 'golden' skippers.

Yealand's remarkable photograph (*see opposite page*) must have required enormous patience to capture. There are several things to look for in the picture. First of all, it clearly shows the broad head of the Skipper family, mentioned already in the commentary on the Chequered Skipper. Secondly, it illustrates clearly the distinctive way in which Skippers hold their wings at an angle to each other, and thirdly it shows the orange tips of the antennae to distinguish it from the Essex Skipper, which has black ends.

Small Skipper

Please don't mock my manic flight,
unless you think I've taken fright –
that's the way a Skipper flies,
unlike other butterflies.

When you hear that rapid whirring,
wings on summer flower-heads stirring,
there's no need to stop and stare;
it's a Skipper in the air.

Just a small one of the clan
will dart as fast as any can.
Perhaps you might just be so kind,
because I have a butterfly mind,
to tolerate my restless ways,
especially on sunny days.

Small Skipper on rampion. Found throughout England and Wales this species has been extending its territory northwards and is now present in the Borders of Scotland.

Small Tortoiseshell

Aglais urticae

The name *Aglais Urticae* was given by the famous Linnaeus in 1758, and is still used today. *Aglais* probably refers to Aglaia, who was the Greek goddess of beauty, splendour, glory, magnificence and adornment. She was one of the three Graces, who often appear dancing in a circle, and was the wife of the god Hephaistos. *Urticae* means 'of the nettles', which arises because the larvae of this butterfly feed on nettles.

It requires some stretching of the visual imagination to see 'tortoiseshell' hues in the wings of the butterfly, but it is very colourful. Its reddish-orange, with black and yellow markings and a ring of blue spots around the edge of the wings, will brighten any day – for me, one day in particular. I was knocked over and broke my thumb skiing in the French Alps a few years ago. It took me a few days to have the nerve to return to the slopes with one hand in plaster. The next day was sunny so I decided to take the cable car up the mountain. I looked at the view for a while, reminded constantly that others were able to ski while I was not, and ended up sitting forlornly at a café overlooking a large precipice. After a few minutes of sipping my cappuccino I saw, to my astonishment, that a butterfly had settled on the table in front of me. So I wrote down what happened, and here it is in the poem. The incident left me glowing with pleasure for the rest of the day, and the next day I plucked up the courage to put on my skis again.

As my sighting of one testifies, Small Tortoiseshell butterflies can appear in some strange places, almost anywhere in the British Isles. They have variable numbers of generations, and are one of the few species to overwinter as adults in Britain. They can sometimes be found hibernating in outbuildings or even indoors. If you find one that has woken from its long sleep in the spring and is trapped in your house, then let it out to find a mate!

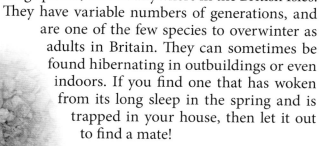

Most of the Small Tortoiseshells we see are born and bred in the UK although in some years significant numbers migrate across the Channel from Europe.

Strong fliers, Small Tortoiseshells can be found almost anywhere in the UK and Ireland, from wet marshes to dry hilltops and urban parks.

Small Tortoiseshell

A butterfly came to me high on the peak –
at two thousand metres it seemed like a freak:
a luminous tortoiseshell red on the snow
had climbed up the world with no further to go.

It flaunted its life at the threat from the cold –
a springtime adventurer dangerously bold
in landscape of nothing but blackness and white
its colours defying the monochrome height.

Its derring-do done it dived over a crag
with an insolent zig and a fluttering zag;

So, butterfly, what was the instinct that drove
a delicate creature to ramble and rove,
your wings in a hurry as if you were late?
It wasn't the view – you were finding a mate!

The underwing of the Small Tortoiseshell has more to do with disguise and camouflage than with display and flamboyance. This one has been tempted to feed on fresh droppings.

Speckled Wood
Pararge aegeria

This is a butterfly that most people should be able to see if they look for one, as it has increased its range and frequency over the last century or so, and in the countryside it is quite common, especially in or near shaded wild areas. It usually has three generations, and the larvae feed on grasses, and can hibernate as either larva or pupa.

The scientific Latin name, *Pararge*, is derived from the Greek words which, taken together, mean 'near to white'. The name was supposedly chosen to indicate the affinity of this butterfly with another of a similar family. In fact it is part of the Satyridae, or Browns, family.

Aegeria was a prophetic nymph, as well as goddess of healing, childbirth and fountains, and so kind, fertile and wet. Pregnant Roman women used to pray to her for a safe and successful birth. She was the lover of Numa Pompilius, second king of Rome, and when he died she was heartbroken and wept so much that the goddess Diana changed her into a spring.

The English name Speckled Wood is much more practically descriptive, as the butterfly is indeed speckled and mainly lives in woodland. Some echo of the Latin name can be perceived in a butterfly that enjoys damp woods occasionally lit by miniature lightning bolts of sunshine descending from the canopy.

A woodland and hedgerow butterfly, the Speckled Wood thrives in sheltered locations where there's dappled sunlight. Uniquely among British butterflies, it can over-winter either as a larva (caterpillar) or pupa (chrysalis).

Speckled Wood

In the dappled edges of the trees
where sunlight spills from leaves
and lingers by the shadows
lives the tawny-ochre Speckled Wood.

It specks and freckles the green-brown air
sometimes luminous, sometimes dark
mingling light and shade
as if dissembling a hidden design.

But when it basks in streams of gold
or plays in dun penumbra
then the Wood seems confident
in its indeterminate guise.

Swallowtail

Papilio machaon

Papilio is the Latin word for butterfly, and this is a very fine one. In the Homeric tale of the Trojan War, *Machaon* was a soldier physician attending to the medical needs of the Greek army, and himself died towards the end of the war. It is not clear why this name was chosen, as the only conceivable therapeutic value provided by this butterfly is likely to be a psychological boost provided by looking at its considerable beauty.

The English name Swallowtail is descriptive, as the insect has long twin tails reminiscent of those of the swallow bird. In modern times the Swallowtail has been confined to small areas of the Norfolk Broads, and it is rare in the sense of being very local. It used to occur much more widely, but its habitat, like that of many butterflies, has shrunk too much. Its larvae eat milk-parsley, and there is one main brood, with a flight period in May to July, and another smaller brood flying in August. They overwinter as pupae.

It is of a slightly different race from its much more widespread close cousins in continental Europe, including France, where the stricken butterfly in this poem was found. In England, it likes fens and marshes, but I have never been there at the right time to see an English Swallowtail. So I decided to write about one in France, where I often see them, sometimes in my own garden in the Languedoc.

The incident described in the poem is similar to one I witnessed in Prague some years ago. I was walking along when I saw an old man several metres ahead of me bend down to touch something on the ground. He appeared to be moving something from the path. I was not close enough to see exactly what he had been doing, but when I reached the relevant spot I discovered a large and sleepy bumble bee in the short grass to one side. The old man had saved the bee from being trampled by a walker.

Male Swallowtails such as this one have wingspans of up to 83mm – a spectacular sight as it flies around the fens and reed beds of the Norfolk Broads.

Swallowtail

In the car park at Leclerc,
a butterfly has landed, dazed
too weak to be fazed
by passing shopping trolleys.

A child lunges for a living toy
but mother pulls away
the small and murderous hand
just in time.

Tyre-tracks in the dust
pass only wing stripes
from the famished Swallowtail.

An old man sees it close to death
and lifts it to a nectar flower,
then watches with his coffee
from the café by the road.

As is feeds and lifts its wings
and flies away
from summery execution
the old man smiles,
enjoys another day.

Swallowtails take nectar from
a variety of plants, including
thistles, teasels, devil's-bit
scabious and clovers. Their
favoured food plants for the
larvae are milk-parsley, fennel
and wild angelica.

Wall Brown

Lasiommata megera

Lasiommata comes from the Greek *lasios*, 'hairy' and *ommata*, 'eyes', as this butterfly has eyes surrounded by minutely fine down. *Megaera* was one of the three Furies, who were female deities of vengeance from the underworld. Classical myth told that they were born from the blood of Uranus when his son Cronos castrated him. After this rather grisly start it is perhaps not surprising that the Furies then spent their time pursuing wrong-doers of all kinds. They were variously depicted with snakes in their hair or with burnt skin and blood-shot eyes, and were described as relentless in their pursuit and torture of their sinful victims.

Megaera specialised in provoking jealousy and punishing marital infidelity and, bearing in mind the inclinations of human nature, she must have been kept busy. In modern French, her name survives as *'mégère'* means a scold or termagant, though even the most fierce *boulangère* beating her straying husband over the head with an overcooked baguette could not equal the nastiness of a Fury in full flight.

The Wall Brown butterfly is utterly inoffensive, enjoying nothing more vengeful than warming itself on stone paths and walls. Its characteristic behaviour is to fly up and resettle restlessly

A Wall warms itself on a drystone wall. It has to raise its body temperature to at least 25ºC before taking flight and it does so by spreading its wings on paths and stones absorbing heat directly from the sun but also reflected from the rock itself.

as a walker passes, hence the poem. It has two generations, with the larvae eating grasses, and overwintering in that form. Adults fly in May to June and July to September very widely in Britain. I have often seen them on coastal paths.

In his photograph on page 165, Yealand has captured an image, very appropriately, of a Wall on a wall. It has flattened itself against the warm stone, with its wings almost clinging to the surface, to raise its temperature before flying off for its pathway dancing. It is as if it has become part of the wall, or painted onto it.

Wall Brown

What is your business, Mr Wall?
Do you have no rest at all?
'Finding flowers and scenting mates;
don't delay me, I'll be late'.

What, then, could be stranger
Than your game with danger?
'I fly around the feet
as a friendly way to greet'.

The summer is short,
and really I ought
before I'm gone
to settle on
a flower
now.

The amazingly well-camouflaged Wall butterfly has declined in numbers and distribution over the past 30 years and scientists speculate this may be due to habitat loss and possibly also climate change. Walls do well in grassland with paths, farm tracks and places with stone walls. They also flourish in areas of limestone pavement.

The Wall is quick to take flight when disturbed. If approached on a path by a walker it seems to be able to sense the movement, shadow or vibration very quickly, prompting it to fly up and on down the path where it may settle again.

White Admiral
Limenitis camilla

White Admirals are butterflies of the English woodlands. I have seen them at the Wetmoor Nature Reserve in Gloucestershire, but they can be seen in many wooded areas. They have a characteristic flight in which they take a few fast flaps of their wings and then glide in and out of low tree branches and shrubs. Their colouring can be surprising, as their upper wings are black and white, but underneath they are orangey-brown and silvery-white. I love to see them gliding, as if sailing over a sea of green and brown. Their caterpillars feed on honeysuckle, woodbine, adding fragrance to their life cycle. They have one brood and fly from June to August, overwintering as larvae.

Aphrodite Limenitis was the Greek mythological protectress of harbours. In the case of this butterfly name she is transformed into Camilla, a legendary warrior maiden, as told by Virgil in his *Aeneid*. She was said to be very fast and adept with a javelin. Camilla was traditionally also a maiden of unblemished character in attendance at religious ceremonies.

Although the name Admiral is probably derived from the same origin here as it is in the naming of Red Admiral, it also seems fitting that a whiter than white protectress of harbours should become a White Admiral in English. The butterfly in my poem, however, never sees the ocean.

A White Admiral basking. Perhaps basking in its own success for it has increased its distribution from just the southern part of England in the early nineteenth century to locations as far north as Lincolnshire and Shropshire.

White Admiral

The sailor who has never seen the sea
pursues a rapid course from tree to tree:
an Admiral of a non-existent fleet
who does not know a tiller from a cleat.

So swoops the admirable Admiral
an altogether landlocked animal,
its white-striped wings like flapping flag hoist code
that points the way along a green-glade road.

The sailors of the Admiral's commands
pay scarce attention to their chief's demands
– a mutiny of Skipper, Blue and White
ignore the distant call to stand and fight.

This Admiral was retired before his birth
and has no need to show a warlike worth;
his bravest task in this his finest hour
is just to decorate a bramble flower.

White Admirals, more than most other British butterflies, like to glide, using their wings intermittently to gain height or change direction. They frequent oak wood clearings and rides where there is wild honeysuckle on which the larvae will feed.

Sir Winston Churchill

Britain's war-time leader is rightly remembered for many reasons, but not usually as a lepidopterist. He enjoyed collecting butterflies as a child at school, and continued his interest during his many travels as a soldier and politician. He is said to have had several favourites, including the Peacock, Small Tortoiseshell, Swallowtail and Painted Lady. At some point he became inspired by the idea of trying to reintroduce to Britain a species of butterfly that had become extinct in this country during the 1920s, the Black-veined White, *Aporia crataegi*.

This is a large and striking butterfly that used to occur in scattered colonies, especially in southern England. One reason why this species appealed especially to Churchill was that Kent, where his country home Chartwell is located, was one of its last remaining strongholds before it finally disappeared from the English countryside. This seems to have called to Churchill's more romantic and nostalgic instincts.

His opportunity came after 1945, when for a few years he was not in office as Prime Minister. At Chartwell he converted an old summer house into a butterfly sanctuary and with the help of experts bred butterflies there. He also stocked his gardens with plants that would attract them, such as buddleia and lavender. Very unfortunately Churchill's attempt to revive the Black-veined White failed, it is said, because his gardener accidentally destroyed the caterpillars when he was pruning hawthorn bushes. It is still not clear whether the butterflies would have survived even if they had pupated and eventually hatched. They would have needed favourable climatic conditions and a wider environment.

In recent years the National Trust (which now owns Chartwell) in conjunction with Butterfly Conservation, has renovated Churchill's butterfly sanctuary and has been breeding indigenous British butterflies for release in the grounds. Since the climate is now warming because of global climate change it is possible that a more successful attempt at reintroducing the Black-veined White could now be made, but modern scientific opinion is wary of such ecological engineering without very careful preparation.

Whites, Large and Small

Pieris brassicae and Pieris rapae

Pieris was Ancient Greek for Muse, of whom, according to legend, there were nine. They were daughters of Zeus, living near Mount Olympus in Greece and were the semi-divine inspirers of creative artists of various kinds. Several of the Muses were specifically connected with the inspiration of poetry. Because of this, I might have been tempted to use pictures of the white butterflies which carry their name for the cover of this book, if they had a more remarkable appearance. Unfortunately, they are some of the least colourful of butterflies.

Either of the Muses Erato or Euterpe could be watching over me as I write, but the butterflies in the countryside around me are also living Muses which can inspire me to compose poetry.

The Large White butterfly also carries the name brassicae, in reference to the cabbage family of plants on which the butterfly larvae feed. The second part of the scientific name for the Small White butterfly is *rapa*, the wild turnip. There are two or three generations and both species overwinter as pupae.

Obviously, Whites are so named because they are white. As far as gardeners are concerned they are just 'Cabbage Whites' and more likely to inspire thoughts of murder than artistic works of beauty. Both of these white species are capable of wreaking terrible destruction on kitchen gardens, but they are themselves victims of parasites and predation by other insects and birds.

A familiar sight to the gardener: the larvae of the Large White enjoying cabbage.

Small Whites can be found almost
everywhere in the British Isles and
they obtain nectar from a wide range
of flowers, from bugle to buddleia, and
ragwort to ragged-robin – or creeping
thistle, as here.

Whites, Large and Small

The very sight of cabbage whites
will give a gardener dreadful frights:
cauliflower's nemesis,
curly kale's doom,
death of purple sprouting
and slaughter of the sprouts
massacre of broccoli
destruction of kohlrabi,
all crucified cruciferae.

They're white, the colour of innocence
with only a few black spots
to advertise their malevolence
guilty of existing, surviving,
of doing what nature demands
and eating leaves of human food,
so, in their anger,
gardeners kill their well-fed babies.

The black edges of forewings of this Large White are longer and more pronounced than they would be on a Small White.

White-letter Hairstreak

Satyrium w-album

Satyrium is a name also borne by the Black Hairstreak and is probably based on the satyrs of Greek mythology, who were half-human goat-like companions of Dionysus. They enjoyed dancing provocatively with nymphs, were usually drunk and had a tendency towards priapism. *W-Album* simply means 'white W'.

The English name shows that it is a butterfly of the Hairstreak family, with streaks on its wings and delicate wing-tails. On the whole it does not resemble a goat with an erection, but it does have a small white 'W' shape on its underwing, hence the name.

It is another of our tragically endangered species, because its larvae feed on the leaves of elm trees that have been decimated by disease in recent decades. The infection had been in Britain since at least the 1920s, but in the late 1960s a more virulent strain appeared. White-letter Hairstreak populations were badly affected, but some of them have clung on to life in the British countryside by finding the few remaining elm survivors, many of which are of the wych-elm variety. More recently there has been evidence that some elms are developing resistance to the disease, and there has been some recovery in the populations of the butterfly.

It has one brood, flying in July and August, and overwinters in the egg stage. I have in the past found adults nectaring on bramble flowers in the Avon Gorge near Bristol, and I hope they still occur there.

**White-letter Hairstreak on a bramble flower.
This butterfly suffered greatly from the effects of
Dutch elm disease, as elm is its larval food plant.**

White-letter Hairstreak

*The White-letter Hairstreak butterfly dwells
in a quite unusual place:
it lurks in the fresh and succulent leaves
on the heights of Wych-Elm trees.*

*The wish of a White-letter Hairstreak is
to discover one of its kin
from preference a creature of opposite sex
who is suitable as a mate.*

*It only descends from high in the leaves
to the bramble-covered rides
at opportune times for mating or meals
or perhaps a little of both.*

*And written behind its tendril-like wing
is a sideways double-you
and only this strange little butterfly knows
what the double-you signifies.*

*It might just as well mean whether as why
if it doesn't mean what or when;
the truth is a mystery strange as the place
where this insect makes its den.*

This specimen clearly shows the white letter 'W' on its hindwing to which it owes its name. The tails exist on both sexes and are thought to be designed to divert attacks from birds.

Wood White
Leptidea sinapis

The scientific name of this butterfly is derived from Greek, meaning a thin, delicate form that feeds on members of the cabbage family. Unlike the 'Cabbage Whites', Wood White larvae in fact feed on plants in the pea and bean family, appropriately named in scientific Latin *Papilionaceae* (meaning leguminous plants whose flowers have butterfly-shaped corollas).

You are unlikely in any case to see one anywhere near cabbages because in Britain the Wood White is rare, restricted to a few places in England and Wales. It has one generation, flying from May to July, and overwinters as a pupa.

Seen in the wild, meandering along a half-shaded woodland ride, perhaps at Symonds Yat in the Wye Valley, the Wood White can look ghostly and flimsy. Its flight seems weak and slow, but graceful and leisurely. At rest it always closes its wings, and it is easily distinguishable from other white butterflies. Of all the British butterflies Wood Whites are perhaps the ones that it is easiest for us to imagine as souls of the dead.

Yealand's photograph (*opposite*) of an individual on a flower of the vetch family wonderfully captures the delicate and ethereal appearance of this modest beauty.

A Wood White mud-puddling. It is attracted to patches of damp ground from which it extracts minerals.

The underside of the ghostly Wood White, a weak flier which survives in the shelter of woodland rides and forestry tracks where common vetch grows.

Wood White

A barely tangible ghost,
it haunts the memory
as well as woodland rides,
seen and unseen, half-imagined
as if a vivid dream
that can barely be recalled –
remarkable but beyond recollection.

A slow-motion trail of existence,
this is no phantasm;
it's the most fragile life
that needs to feed and mate
and survive human poisons.
If it were a spectre it could never die,
but it lives and suffers.

The Wood White has a slow, relentless way of flying, seldom rising more than a yard or two above the ground, and rarely settling once the sun is up. But when it does alight it can be distinguished from other 'Whites' by the fact that it will always have closed wings at rest.